THE DREAM

Breaking Champions League Records

CARLO ANCELOTTI
WITH CHRIS BRADY

EBURY
SPOTLIGHT

EBURY SPOTLIGHT

UK | USA | Canada | Ireland | Australia
India | New Zealand | South Africa

Ebury Spotlight is part of the Penguin Random House group of companies whose addresses can be found at global.penguinrandomhouse.com

Penguin Random House UK
One Embassy Gardens, 8 Viaduct Gardens, London SW11 7BW

penguin.co.uk
global.penguinrandomhouse.com

First published by Ebury Spotlight in 2025

1

Copyright © Carlo Ancelotti and Chris Brady 2025
The moral right of the author has been asserted.

No part of this book may be used or reproduced in any manner for the purpose of training artificial intelligence technologies or systems. In accordance with Article 4(3) of the DSM Directive 2019/790, Penguin Random House expressly reserves this work from the text and data mining exception.

Image credits: Getty Images / Staff (Image 1); Cesare Galimberti / Olycom (Image 2); Guerin Sportivo, 26 April – 2 May, 1989 (Image 3); Bob Thomas / Contributor / Getty Images (Images 4, 5); Alessandro Sabattini / Contributor / Getty Images (Images 6, 7); FILIPPO MONTEFORTE / Staff / Getty Images (Image 8); Shaun Botterill / Staff / Getty Images (Image 9); Boris Streubel / Contributor / Getty Images (Image 10); Alexander Hassenstein – UEFA / Contributor (Image 11); NurPhoto / Contributor / Getty Images (Image 12); Antonio Villalba / Contributor / Getty Images (Image 13); Denis Doyle / Stringer / Getty Images (Image 14); Michael Regan – UEFA / Contributor / Getty Images (Image 15); Mateusz Slodkowski / Contributor / Getty Images (Image 16)

Typeset in 11.8/17.4pt New Baskerville ITC Pro by Six Red Marbles UK, Thetford, Norfolk
Printed and bound in Great Britain by Clays Ltd, Elcograf S.p.A.

The authorised representative in the EEA is Penguin Random House Ireland, Morrison Chambers, 32 Nassau Street, Dublin D02 YH68

A CIP catalogue record for this book is available from the British Library

HARDBACK ISBN 9781529955569
TRADE PAPERBACK ISBN 9781529955576

Penguin Random House is committed to a sustainable future for our business, our readers and our planet. This book is made from Forest Stewardship Council® certified paper.

To Mariann

Contents

Introduction   1

PART ONE: THE DREAMING BEGINS

Chapter One: When in Roma, 1983–4   7

Chapter Two: Just One Scudetto, 1987–8   13

Chapter Three: The First Time, 1988–9   21

Chapter Four: The Second Time, 1989–90   33

PART TWO: LEAN YEARS

Chapter Five: Mr Somebody, 1990–5   49

Chapter Six: A League of Its Own, 1995–2001   59

PART THREE: MILAN – THE COACHING YEARS

Chapter Seven: Christmas Comes Early, 2001–2   69

Chapter Eight: The Third Time, 2002–3   81

Chapter Nine: From La Coruña . . . to Istanbul 2003–5   97

Chapter Ten: The Fourth Time, 2005–7   115

CONTENTS

Chapter Eleven: Blue Is the Colour, 2007–11   143

Chapter Twelve: Je Ne Regrette Rien, 2011–13   163

PART FOUR: MADRID

Chapter Thirteen: The Fifth Time, 2013–14   179

Chapter Fourteen: Der Wanderer, 2014–19   201

Chapter Fifteen: The Sixth Time, 2019–22   221

Chapter Sixteen: The Seventh Time, 2022–4   249

Epilogue   277
Appendix   285
Acknowledgements   297

Introduction

DREAMS

I want to begin this story in an unexpected place. It's a football game, yes, but between two unusual teams. Both of them were captained by great Italian film directors, Bernardo Bertolucci and Pier Paolo Pasolini. Both were filming near my home. They had been friends but had fallen out. To restore the friendship, it was suggested that they should have a game of football between the two film crews. Bertolucci had a smaller group to choose from and needed a couple of players to make up the numbers. It was March 1975, and I was only 15. I played centre-forward and was on Parma's youth team back then. When we finished our game on the Saturday we were invited to play in a pick-up game the next day. Pasolini was told that we were newly recruited toolmakers to work on set. I don't think anyone believed it. The plan worked: football had brought them together again. We won and Bertolucci thanked us all because our contribution had been decisive.

To be honest, the names Bertolucci and Pasolini didn't mean much to me. But I didn't care, it was a game, and I

THE DREAM

just wanted to play. Football was already my life. I dreamed of playing, all the things a kid does – and luckily for me, it came true. Almost exactly fifty years ago, I was on that pitch at the Cittadella and from there I've been round the world, running after a ball, chasing my football dreams.

It was always my dream from as early as I can remember. To be a footballer. To play professional football in Italy. I grew up on a farm in Emilia-Romagna, north of the Apennines, south of the Alps. There wasn't much money, and what there was came from the sale of parmigiano – the Parmesan cheese that is the region's world-famous product.

I didn't think about becoming world-famous. I just wanted to play the game.

Sure enough, that dream became a reality. And then came another dream – to play for the best team in Europe.

The odds on becoming a professional footballer are very long as it is. But to be associated with a team that conquers a whole continent? That happens to very few. Somehow, though, it has happened for me. First as a player, then as a manager. I won the European Cup twice with AC Milan in consecutive years (1989, then 1990). A couple of years later the competition changed its shape and its name. Previously a knockout cup with each tie played over two legs, it took on a new guise as the Champions League. This was much harder to win, because you had to play many more games.

That summer I retired, so I never competed in the new-look cup as a player. But it was to become the dominant

INTRODUCTION

competition in my life as a manager. Year after year, season after season, it was the ultimate goal, the prize at the end of the rainbow. The dream. At the top level, each season the Champions League stands apart as separate from the league title race. It is akin to a military campaign. Its success or failure colours the memory of the entire season. Somehow, I would go on to win the Champions League five times as a manager. It is amazing to me that no one else, as a player and a manager, has won Europe's premier competition more. I won two European Cups alongside fantastic team-mates, and then had the privilege of coaching some of the best players in the world, lifting those five Champions League trophies in the process. The list of stars who I have had the honour to work with looks like a Who's Who of international football from the past 40 years. Don't ask me to pick my best eleven from such a galaxy. I couldn't possibly do it!

This is the story of how my dream came true a magnificent seven times. But it's also the story of all the many more occasions when it proved beyond my grasp. Football is not so far removed from the rest of life. The reality is that most of the time you don't win. And I hope I am humble enough to understand that defeat can be a great teacher too.

But when you do beat everyone else, the satisfaction is indescribable. All the same, I will try to capture the feeling in words.

PART ONE
THE DREAMING BEGINS

1

WHEN IN ROMA, 1983–4

Some players are lucky enough to create incredible memories from their first encounter with the European Cup. They get all the way to the final and have the eyes of the whole continent upon them. Their team wins. They may even score. And the experience gives them something to treasure for the rest of their lives.

That is not how *my* story started.

The first time I experienced a European Cup final was as a frustrated spectator. I was a young player at AS Roma as we advanced through the tournament. To my great disappointment, I got injured and missed the semi-final, and then the final too. Perhaps I wouldn't have minded quite so much if this hadn't been a home game for us. The final was scheduled to take place at the Stadio Olimpico in Rome. That brought an extra dimension to the game. The yellow-and-red half of the city, the Giallorossi, was overwhelmed by this opportunity for their club to win the biggest club competition in its own backyard.

THE DREAM

The truth is that back in the 1980s, although the European competition was growing in importance – at least in Italy – it wasn't as important as Serie A. Winning the league championship – *lo Scudetto*, as we call it in Italy – was always the greater test and the bigger prize. To reach the European Cup final you had to get through only eight games – four home and away legs – and the first two rounds were usually against the champions of less prestigious leagues. In Roma's case we overcame the champions of Sweden, Bulgaria and East Germany, all by aggregate margins of two goals. But it was the identity of our opponents in the semi-finals that tells you how different things were back then. We took on the Scottish team Dundee United. The Scottish title was almost always won by either Celtic or Rangers, apart from a brief period of disruption when Alex Ferguson won it three times with Aberdeen before he headed south to Manchester United. Like us, Dundee United were competing in the European Cup for the first time. We lost 2–0 away in Scotland but won 3–0 at home, so we were on our way to the final.

Roma was coached by Nils Liedholm, who had a big influence on my career. I'd led a sheltered life growing up in the Po Valley and had never spent this much time with a foreigner before. He was Swedish, but as a young man he had been a big player for AC Milan, where he acquired the nickname *Il Barone*. The story goes that he was so precise and reliable a passer that when after several seasons he

WHEN IN ROMA, 1983–4

finally misplaced a ball they gave him a standing ovation at the San Siro.

He had a strange career as a coach in the merry-go-round of Italian football. He ended up being the head coach of AC Milan four times, and Roma four times too. That must be some kind of record. His importance to me was that in 1979, during his second stint as manager of Roma, he stopped off in nearby Parma on his way back from a holiday in Salsomaggiore, a spa town at the foot of the Apennines, to sign me. I was just turning 20 and at that time was still playing as a striker. It was his idea to convert me into a midfielder, and I instantly felt much more at ease. In those early years he took me under his wing and devoted a lot of time to giving me tactical advice and pep talks on not only technique but life skills that would prove useful out in the wider world.

He was my first proper coach, and I learned from him that a boss doesn't need to be someone who throws his weight around and sternly lays down the rules. He was quiet – I never heard him shout, not even once. In his humility and aura of calm he reminded me a little bit of my father, who wouldn't lose his temper even when the harvest was going badly. He was flexible about things like timekeeping and diet. Most of all he was relaxed about tactics, trusting his players to think independently on the pitch. He also had a formidable sense of humour and used it to defuse any pressure and tension. I remember once when I was sitting in a car with two teammates and two women, Liedholm came out of the hotel where we were staying to go for a stroll. He walked over, looking suspicious. Of course, many other managers would have told us off and probably sent us to our rooms. The window was wound down. He looked in and asked, 'Is there a bit of room for me too?'

The second non-Italian to catch my attention was Roma's latest purchase, the great midfielder Paulo Roberto Falcão. There were two Brazilians in the team: Tino Cerezo was more of a battler and a workhorse; Falcão was a brilliant playmaker and a leader on the pitch. And it was on the training ground that Falcão also brought fresh ideas. When he arrived, he couldn't understand why we did so much training without the ball. Maybe this sort of exchange happened everywhere else in Europe as South American players started to arrive in bigger numbers, but it was at Roma that I came under the direct influence of a Brazilian genius as well as a Swedish mastermind.

That said, Liedholm probably got our preparation wrong for the final. The league had finished so we were free to decamp from Rome and spend a week in the mountains. The idea was to focus our attention on the game, keep us relaxed and get out of the cauldron that was starting to bubble over in anticipation of hosting the biggest club game on the planet in our home city. But looking back, maybe the break in our normal routine was the opposite of relaxing. The atmosphere in the mountains was different and unfortunately so was the weather. It was cold and wet, unlike the

WHEN IN ROMA, 1983–4

city, which was hot when we got back there. It may explain why, when the game went into extra time, a lot of my teammates suffered from cramp.

But I was already injured so had to sit out the game as we took on the might of Liverpool, who had won it three times in recent seasons. After two hours of stalemate, the match finished 1–1, which meant a penalty shoot-out. Teams didn't practise penalties so much back then and it showed.

With the benefit of hindsight and long experience, I now know that penalty shoot-outs are 100 per cent psychological. You can practise them all day at the training ground, but you are wasting your time. Any player good enough to play for a top team can score a penalty. The question is, can they do it with the world watching them? And I am afraid that there is only one way to find out. Right at the start of my career, I took a penalty for Roma in the shoot-out in the 1980 Coppa Italia final against Torino. Mine was the first of the sudden-death penalties and I scored. I was 20 years old and remember running up to the ball thinking, *I am putting this to the goalkeeper's right*. It went in, but it went in to his left. You can think and plan but sometimes an instinct takes over. We won that shoot-out. Would we win this one?

Players from both sides shot the ball over the bar, but more of ours than theirs. To stay in contention, we had to score with our fifth penalty kick. Forty years on I can still picture the Liverpool keeper, Bruce Grobbelaar, standing on his line and wobbling his legs as if they'd turned to jelly – 'spaghetti legs', I think the English media called them. If he was trying to put off my senior team-mate Francesco Graziani, it worked. His shot clipped the top of the bar and flew over. Depending on your view of it, it remains one of the most famous or infamous moments in the entire history of penalty shoot-outs.

Roma lost. Liverpool won their fourth European Cup. In the end I think the pressure of hosting the final was too much. The final moved to a different stadium every year, as the Champions League final does now. But it very rarely happens that it's a home game for one of the finalists. Before 1984 it had happened only twice, with Real Madrid in 1957 and Inter Milan in 1965. And since then, there has been just Bayern Munich in 2012. All those clubs knew their way around the competition. Perhaps there was extra intensity for Roma because it was the club's first ever European Cup campaign. The expectation and the pressure were just too much. As things stand, it turns out to have been their only final of the premier European cup competition.

It was a painful night to be a spectator. As I looked on helplessly from my seat, I was not to know that, many years later, Liverpool would provide the opposition for two of the most memorable nights of my life.

So that was my first acquaintance with the European Cup. My next came after I had left Roma.

2

JUST ONE SCUDETTO, 1987–8

Milan felt a very natural destination for me. Although like Rome it was a big city, it wasn't so very far from where I grew up. So I was happy to hear that AC Milan were interested in me in the close season of 1987. To be specific, their new coach Arrigo Sacchi was interested in me. After the departure of Ray Wilkins, he needed a new central midfielder.

It was a sliding doors moment for me, because Ray would later be an important figure by my side when I went to England to manage Chelsea. But for now Sacchi wanted a more mobile player to replace him. Unfortunately, club president Berlusconi and the general manager, Adriano Galliani, had their doubts about how mobile I actually was. My knees weren't what they used to be after several injuries and they worried they'd be buying a crock. The club doctor who gave me my medical was worried too. Sacchi was persuasive. I remember Berlusconi saying, 'I cannot sign Ancelotti, the doctor says he is 20 per cent less mobile in his knee after his last operation. He had a meniscus problem; it was operated on many times.' Sacchi responded as only he could. 'If I sign Ancelotti we will win the league. I do not care if he is 20 per cent less mobile in the knee. I would only worry if he were 20 per cent less mobile in the mind.'

That seemed to do the trick.

The incredible thing is that Sacchi came to this conclusion about my abilities without once having spoken to me before he signed me. He had gathered as much information about my character as he could. When he was still coaching at Parma he had asked for intelligence about me, and he sent a scout to watch how I trained at Roma, to see how hard I was prepared to work. Obviously, he was satisfied with what he had been told.

But, even for Sacchi, I was by no means the finished article. According to Berlusconi, I played like an orchestra director who couldn't read sheet music. Sacchi reassured him that he would teach me how to conduct. In practice that meant coming in an hour earlier to train with some kids from the youth team. That way, he told the boss, we would go through everything.

The point of promising to win the league was that AC Milan would then qualify to play in the European Cup. This was Berlusconi's dream. The club had recent knowledge of the doldrums. He had bought Milan only the previous year, saving it from bankruptcy in the process. Having last won the Scudetto in 1979, it had since spent time in Serie B

JUST ONE SCUDETTO, 1987–8

(1980–1 and 1982–3, the only times in its history). So it was quite ambitious of the club's president to think he could make AC Milan into a superclub to rival Liverpool, Juventus, Real Madrid and Bayern Munich. It looks as if I was a jigsaw piece in that project.

Roma didn't want me to leave, and only agreed to let AC Milan talk to me at the last minute so that my registration papers had to be sped by private jet and motorbike courier to the league headquarters.

Sacchi was a new arrival himself. My old Roma boss Nils Liedholm had just been let go by AC Milan. His replacement was an unusual figure in Italian football. Sacchi never played the game professionally and for some of his life worked as a shoe salesman. As a coach he was still in his thirties when he had success with Parma, which got him noticed by Berlusconi. Unimpressed by his credentials, the media dubbed him Signor Nessuno. Mr Nobody.

The team assembled by Sacchi would become known in the Italian press as 'The Immortals'. In 2007 *World Soccer* magazine asked a global panel of experts to name the greatest team of all time. Pelé's Brazil side that won the World Cup in 1970 finished top of the list. Then came the Hungarians, led by Ferenc Puskás, who famously ripped England apart in 1953. The Netherlands side that lost the World Cup final in 1974 came third. The highest-placed club side, in fourth, was Sacchi's AC Milan.

Why were they – we – so good?

THE DREAM

We had our captain, Franco Baresi. He was a lion at the heart of defence. He had an incredible strength and a fantastic work ethic, and great technical skill – he was a genuine ball player as well as an indomitable stopper. But most of all, with those cool blue eyes of his, he had a powerful aura of authority. This didn't show in his manner off the pitch, when he was quite quiet. But out there in the thick of the action his voice came through loud and clear.

Baresi was the most important building block of the side. From him everything flowed. But it helped that Sacchi mixed a strong Dutch element into his squad of Italians. Dutch players were brought up on the total football of the 1970s, a style that encouraged flexibility and freedom of expression. There was also a culture in the Netherlands of players speaking their minds. The Dutch like an argument. This sometimes created problems in the Dutch national team, where the senior players seemed to be more in charge than the coach, but it worked for us. That summer two tall Dutchmen arrived who would form a potent force up front – Ruud Gullit and Marco van Basten. Van Basten was an incredible technician, while Gullit in particular was a very strong character, a leader and a motivator.

Gullit's qualities were important because Baresi could be quiet in the dressing room. Even on the pitch he was not loud, but he had a presence. People saw him as just a *libero*, a sweeper, perhaps because he was only 1.77m, but he was also dominant in the air. He was an all-round defender

JUST ONE SCUDETTO, 1987–8

who would definitely thrive in today's game, as he would in any era. Roberto Donadoni, a great wide player, quick and defensively aware, joined at the same time. The exciting young left back Paolo Maldini was another giant in the making. A year later our Netherlands contingent grew to three with the arrival of Frank Rijkaard, a player who mixed power with skill as a defensive midfielder.

In central midfield I was cast as a chief of staff who brought his intellect onto the pitch. As battlefield commander in the thick of the action, my job was very specific, and it involved a lot of hard work. Sacchi referred to my ability to cover so much of the pitch 'without the need to be a beast physically'. I think he meant that I lacked pace.

The demands put on me by Sacchi were greater than anything I'd known at Roma. I was to be the link between Baresi at the centre of defence and Gullit, who roamed at the base of the attack. Sacchi had a system and we three were its spine. His tactics have since been adopted by many coaches, but in the late 1980s they were innovative, even revolutionary, particularly in Italian football. In fact, he completely changed Italian football in every way imaginable, both in terms of training and tactics and above all the level and pace at which the game was played. The emphasis had always been on defending. Sacchi's philosophy was to defend by attacking.

Sacchi got rid of the traditional Italian *libero* and introduced zonal marking in two defensive lines of four. Baresi's

THE DREAM

abilities enabled this transition to be accomplished without too much upheaval. We practised this without let-up. In reducing the distance between the defence and the front line, his idea was to squeeze the space in which the opposition could play. Then when we did get possession, he wanted us to use it with rapid penetration. Baresi kept a high line at the heart of defence while Gullit was a big and mobile striker who never stopped roaming. As the conduit in that trio, I had to do a lot of running. Sacchi insisted that the three of us were never too far from one another, to the extent that in training he would tie the three of us to a length of rope in order to get us used to the idea that we had to maintain precise distances. This sounds insane when I write it down, and it definitely felt so at the time. But look at the results. After three seasons playing the Sacchi way, I had dropped 6 kilograms and won one Scudetto and two European Cups.

The first of those was won in my first year there. In 1987–8 the Serie A season went down to the wire. The decider, in effect, was the game that took us to Naples, where we were to play Napoli, the reigning champions, in the threatening atmosphere of Stadio San Paolo. We had beaten them 4–1 at home in a game that galvanised our season and by the start of May we were second in the league and only a point behind. Napoli were led by their captain and talisman Diego Maradona, who since his arrival at the start of the 1984–5 season had helped to bring them their first ever title. And he was now enjoying what he later described as his greatest ever season. 'I don't want to

JUST ONE SCUDETTO, 1987–8

see a single Milan flag at the San Paolo,' he said before the game. 'We are at home and for them it must be like a graveyard. Here they must die. I want to see the San Paolo all blue.' The stadium holds 82,000, so that was a lot of blue.

The game is often described as one of the greatest in Serie A history. It was the perfect finale – top-of-the-league reigning champions Napoli versus second-placed Milan. The champions versus the challengers.

The first goal arrived after about 30 minutes. I was a long way from goal when I picked up the ball 60 or 70 yards from Napoli's goal. When I looked up there was space in front of me, so I went into it and just kept going. It was like the sea had parted before me; no Napoli player came to me until I was brought down just outside their penalty area. I touched the free kick to Evani on my left and he fired in a shot that deflected off the wall but straight into the path of the alert Pietro Paolo Virdis, who slid the ball past the onrushing keeper. Two minutes before half-time, Maradona equalised with a tremendous 20-yard free kick into the top left-hand corner of the net. Not unexpected, but how do you stop Maradona? Gullit tried, leaping up at the far end of the wall, and nearly got his head to the ball. Maradona later claimed that he deliberately aimed to clip the top of Gullit's famous dreadlocks.

Maradona was undoubtedly the greatest footballer I ever played against. He was so difficult to stop and had amazing strength and speed to go with his unbelievable skill. In that game he pulled off an incredible rabona pass, to the

THE DREAM

Brazilian striker Careca. My main solution for keeping him in check was strong contact, but he never complained. In fact, after we finished playing we became good friends at the many events where we would bump into each other. He was very humble and, despite all the controversies surrounding his life, he is such a big loss for football. Maradona also seemed to respect me as a player. 'Arrigo,' he once said to Sacchi, 'under you Ancelotti runs fast.' 'He doesn't run fast,' my coach replied. 'He thinks fast.' Two of the game's greats talking fondly about me: it doesn't get much better than that.

But, back to the game. We needed to win so Sacchi replaced Donadoni with Van Basten at half-time and moved Gullit centrally. From that moment on, we were on top. Or rather Gullit was on top. He terrorised the Napoli back line, setting up two goals, first from the right, then from the left. Like Maradona, when a great player is playing well, he is difficult to stop. Gullit was a great player. From the right, he provided the perfect cross for Virdis to head in our second goal, and we were back in front. Then he went in for the kill, appearing in space on the left, bursting past retreating defenders before calmly rolling the ball into the path of Van Basten, who smashed his shot into an empty net. People forget how quick Gullit was – it was a lightning counter-attack. 3–1 to Milan and game over. It turned out that the Scudetto was also over, not just the game, as Napoli failed to win either of their final two games. We were in the Champions League, and we thought we were ready. It would soon be time to find out.

3
THE FIRST TIME, 1988-9

It had been more than four years since my last experience with the European Cup, and even then it was only as a spectator while injured at Roma. Now, in the autumn of 1988, I found myself watching from the wings once again. Only this time it wasn't an injury that kept me off the pitch. It was indiscipline.

Let me explain. Arrigo Sacchi's AC Milan announced itself in Europe's premier competition with an easy win against the Bulgarian champions Levski Sofia. On 6 October we brushed them aside at home with four goals from Marco van Basten. For the next few years our Dutch frontman was going to demoralise defenders all over Europe, and the 1988-9 season was just the start. He and Ruud Gullit were now joined at Milan by their compatriot Frank Rijkaard. Their confidence, sky-high already, had been turbo-boosted over the summer as the Netherlands finally fulfilled all that national promise and won the European Championships, hosted in West Germany. (I and three of my Milan team-mates played in the Italian team, which lost in a rainy semi-final to the Soviet Union.)

After Levski Sofia came a more difficult hurdle. Red Star Belgrade were representing Yugoslavia in that season's competition. They were no pushover, having some very special players in their squad who would themselves go on to win the competition in 1991. The Montenegrin midfielder Dejan Savićević would finish joint runner-up in the Ballon d'Or, behind Jean-Pierre Papin of Marseille, and move to AC Milan. The blond Croatian midfielder Robert Prosinečki would win best young player at the 1990 FIFA World Cup and go on to play for both Real Madrid and Barcelona. But most of all there was Dragan Stojković, a true general who could weave subtle patterns in the heart of the midfield. He also had a wily ability to get under your skin, and he had done just that to me at the San Siro.

We had an argument after that first leg, at the end of which he said to me, 'I'll be waiting for you in Belgrade.' The game finished 1–1. Stojković opened the scoring at the start of the second half with a clever mazy dribble before slipping a shot inside the near post. The Yugoslavs celebrated wildly because, even though we equalised a minute later, an away goal back then was twice as valuable. It was a spicy encounter, and I became one of five players whose names entered the referee's book. That would prove significant.

Two weeks later we were in Belgrade. Red Star's stadium is intimidating at the best of times, and with that away goal

THE FIRST TIME, 1988–9

of theirs we knew it would be hard to subdue them. But I was determined not to be overawed. As we lined up in the tunnel, I found Stojković and had a word. 'I am here,' I said to him, 'and now we are going to play.' I'm not sure if he understood my Italian but my gestures that accompanied my words made my thoughts clear.

We walked out onto the pitch and almost my first act after the whistle blew was to earn myself another yellow card. The person I got booked for fouling? No prizes for guessing – Stojković. It was our first contact of the game. Meanwhile my team-mate Virdis got himself sent off and we conceded a goal. Our team were staring down the barrel – not only a goal and an away goal behind, but down to 10 men. Elimination for an AC Milan side who would go on to be dubbed the Immortals looked very likely at this point.

But then we were saved in the most dramatic fashion. A thick fog descended and enveloped the whole pitch. Apparently autumn fog is not unusual in that part of the world, but this was exceptional. Visibility wasn't perfect at the kick-off, but in the second half it became difficult to make out the players nearby, let alone those in the distance. I'm sure the crowd could hardly see anything. If you look back at the coverage today on YouTube, it's amazing that the camera crew knew which way to point their equipment. Eventually, not long after Savićević scored early in the second half, the tie had to be abandoned. Call it luck, or fate, or divine intervention.

THE DREAM

Even though the match was abandoned, my second yellow card in the competition was not. It meant that when we came back 24 hours later to resume the second leg, I was not eligible to play and had to sit in the stand and watch. Sacchi was so furious that he fined me.

I was one of the lucky ones. My team-mate Roberto Donadoni was also missing from the second game for a much more serious reason. Incredibly, in the replay of that abandoned game he had nearly died. It happened when he and Red Star's Vasilijevic clashed in midair. Vasilijevic hit Roberto with everything – head, elbow, force.

The impact knocked Donadoni out and for a few scary moments he seemed to be having convulsions. His complexion changed colour and his skin turned sort of blue. Luckily, Red Star's doctor, with the help of our club masseur, probably saved his life. If my memory is right, I think the doctor had to forcibly, manually break Donadoni's jawbone and pull his tongue loose or he would have choked to death. Donadoni then began to stamp his feet on the ground, which can apparently be a symptom of a serious head injury.

The rest of us were traumatised and reacted in different ways. Van Basten was in tears and didn't want to play on. If that game had been played today, it would have been abandoned there and then. Roberto went straight to hospital; as play continued, we had no idea how he was. There was a loudspeaker announcement – Paolo Maldini told me afterwards that he will always be grateful to one of the Red Star players who translated

THE FIRST TIME, 1988–9

the Serbian announcement and let him know that Roberto was OK. Paolo passed on the good news to the rest of us.

As you would expect, with our team-mate in hospital the rest of us had an uncomfortable night. We had to sleep, but it was difficult to not think about how frightened we were for our friend. Every footballer wants to win matches, but this was something different and more important than the game. In that sense it was a really complicated night for us.

Luckily for me, and for Virdis, our behaviour was not punished by the result of the replayed game. In the first half Van Basten scored with an imperious far-post header, before the inevitable Stojković, released down the left by Savićević, burst through our defence and equalised four minutes later with a first-time left-foot drive. Although Van Basten scored another goal that was clearly a metre over the line, the referee and linesman had no access to VAR back then and disallowed it. Nothing else could divide the two teams and I found myself once again watching nervously from the stand as my team participated in a penalty shoot-out. It was our leader Baresi who set the template for us, ramming the first penalty into the roof of the net. We scored all of ours, while our keeper Giovanni Galli made two saves. We were through.

What a strange and dramatic week that was. Such a situation would not have happened today. But without the fog there might have been no story to tell about AC Milan and my Champions League dream. It's not as if I needed the extra motivation, but the club did promise to cancel my fine if we went on to win the European Cup.

Then came Werder Bremen. We had two really tight games against them. In the first leg in West Germany the most clear-cut chances fell to Van Basten. A corner was flicked to him at the far post, where he headed the ball powerfully down. It bounced around like a pinball off the Bremen players, then against the underside of the crossbar, until someone cleared it. It was definitely over the line and goal-line technology would surely confirm that nowadays. To be fair Bremen also had a goal disallowed for a foul on our goalkeeper which, now that I think about it, was no foul at all.

The home leg back in Milan was tense, but we felt in control. Van Basten won it for us with a penalty, and we were through to the semi-final of the European Cup.

This was where the competition got really serious. Our opponents were Real Madrid. It was exactly the sort of tie our president wanted us to be a part of, because Real was the club he measured Milan against. In playing them in the semi-final, he could see how far we had progressed in the short span of time since Sacchi took over. This would be the greatest test for his project. In reality, it was more like the final he wanted. I say this partly because when we looked at the other semi-final – Steaua Bucharest vs Galatasaray – we thought that we could beat both of those teams but Real Madrid would be different. They were the toughest side left

THE FIRST TIME, 1988–9

in the competition and, if we got past them, you could argue that we already had one hand on the trophy.

Real were the aristocrats of European football. They had won the competition more than any other club, including five straight titles in the first five years of its existence. They were barely less powerful in the second half of the 1980s. Perhaps they had not won the European Cup in a while, but this was their third straight semi-final, and they were well on their way to a fourth consecutive La Liga title. The stars of their current side played together up front. The Spanish striker Emilio Butragueño was partnered by the Mexican poacher Hugo Sánchez, who had a phenomenal scoring rate of 208 goals in 282 games for Real. Behind them was the blond West German playmaker Bernd Schuster.

The first leg in Madrid was a good game. It was more open than anyone expected and, in the first half especially, we were on top, so much so that even Baresi was making forward breaks. One time he broke up the left and his pass, inside the penalty area, found Maldini. It was as if our entire formation had been turned on its head. I remember wondering what the hell the two of them were doing up there. Maybe it was the Dutch influence: total football being demonstrated by two born-and-bred Milanesi.

Despite everything, we went behind just before half-time. It was a bad one to concede as it exposed a strange lack of marking. A corner flew in from the left where it was flicked on to Sánchez, who finished on the volley from six yards.

THE DREAM

No one was anywhere near either Madrid player. Sánchez was an early adopter of the gymnastic goal celebration and launched into one of his spectacular flips. We were keen to ensure that he didn't get the chance for any more acrobatics.

We kept them at bay in the second half while we went looking for the all-important away goal. It came out of nowhere with 15 minutes to go. It was certainly worth the wait. Our right back, Mauro Tassotti, was drifting upfield when he spotted Van Basten on the edge of the box. Strangely unchallenged, Tassotti was free to drift a curling cross for Van Basten to make something of. It wasn't a great ball to be honest, aimed towards the penalty spot and coming in at not much more than waist height: too high to volley, it was probably too low to head. But Van Basten really attacked the ball, darting towards it and, to the surprise of the covering defender, stooped to hook his neck around the ball. His diving header had so much power from that far out that it looped over the keeper, hit the underside of the cross bar and bounced down over the line. Only Van Basten could score such a goal.

There were plenty of chances at both ends, but the game finished 1–1 and so we had the hard-won treasure of an away goal. When we returned to Milan, we knew that we had to be ready to protect our advantage.

We did it the Sacchi way. That second leg might well be seen as the moment when the greatness of that Milan team was first acknowledged by the football world, and I was proud and thrilled to be part of it. Sacchi played me slightly

THE FIRST TIME, 1988–9

more forward than usual and told me that he was confident in my ability to 'adapt to any position'. His confidence gave me confidence, of course.

It was against Real that we really started to press more than any other team. Sacchi's philosophy was that to defend the ball you must attack the ball when the other team is in possession, no matter where that might be on the pitch. It was far from normal practice in Italy, where *catenaccio* was still the default way of playing. In that system, once the opponent has control of the ball you would retreat in a funnel towards your own goal. Our new system relied on an intensity that took our opponents by surprise.

Madrid could not cope with such intensity. I have been told that they gave up the ball to us 48 times in that match. I am not sure if that is true, but I know they found the going tough and definitely gave it away a lot. I think that Real Madrid at that time really didn't know that we could play like this. There was not a lot of information at the time. What we were doing was totally new to them. Perhaps we were helped by the fact that in the 1980s there was much less ability to analyse foreign opponents in detail before a game. This was the pre-Moneyball age, when not every game was shown on satellite channels, so the coaches had less access to statistical assistance.

The confidence that Sacchi had given me translated into one of the best goals of my entire career. It happened like this. In the 17th minute Gullit got caught in a lot of traffic out on the right wing. He had four Madrid players around him, but he somehow weaved a path through them and found me just in front of the centre circle. The midfield was less crowded because half of our opponents had been clustered around Gullit. But Schuster was in front of me, and I showed him the ball before wrong-footing him as I moved to my right. I did exactly the same to the next player. Suddenly there was no one to stop me letting off a shot. It was a long way out – probably 30 yards – but I hit the ball as hard as I could. To watch it sail over the back four and the outstretched right hand of the goalkeeper, who was quite far off his line, and into the roof of the net was a spectacular feeling. I was capable of hitting the ball hard from that sort of distance, but to do so at such an important moment felt very special. I could barely believe it and set off in ecstasy towards the dugout, only to be smothered by my team-mates before I could get there. The Hollywood stuff was mostly done by others in the team. So to make a contribution with that goal in such a game meant a great deal to me.

The three Dutch masters had immense physical and aerial power and once they got going they were very difficult for any side to contain, even Real Madrid; they terrified the Madrid defence. Rijkaard scored first with a majestic header. Then Gullit glanced in a header from almost the same position. In the second half the three of them combined in a triangular masterpiece. Rijkaard floated a chip forward towards Gullit, who headed it down into the path of Van

THE FIRST TIME, 1988–9

Basten, who dinked the ball onto his left foot and drilled it into the roof of the net. They were unstoppable that night.

The wonderful icing on the cake was that my friend Donadoni had fully recovered from his ordeal in Belgrade and scored our fifth and final goal. He took a corner on the right, exchanged a pass with a team-mate and dribbled towards the right-hand edge of the box, then with his left foot fired a low grasscutter inside the near post.

That night at the San Siro remains the worst ever defeat of Real Madrid in either version of the competition. The only result that matches it came against Kaiserslautern in 1982, but in that game, they had three men sent off. They had no such excuse against us.

If any further evidence that Sacchi knew exactly what he was doing was needed, it was provided by the final. It was held at the Camp Nou in Barcelona, which was filled with 90,000 of our fans. I still remember every detail of the atmosphere. Our opponents were Steaua Bucharest, whose fans were unable to travel out of communist Romania. (Everything changed in Eastern Europe later on in 1989, but that is another story.) With the odds so stacked in our favour, it seemed impossible for us to lose, and so it proved.

Everything fell into place. Sacchi favoured a very disciplined 4–4–2 formation but when you looked around the dressing room you would think that with these players you could probably play in any position, in any system. It just so happened that the make-up of the team made us perfectly

THE DREAM

suited to 4–4–2. Galli was safe in goal and the back four of Tassotti, Baresi, Costacurta and Maldini was close to flawless. Between them they would go on to play over 2,800 times for AC Milan. That statistic will surely never be matched. In midfield the flank players were Donadoni and Angelo Colombo along with myself and Rijkaard in the centre. Up front, Gullit and Van Basten. Not bad. Certainly too good for Steaua Bucharest, even with their star man Gheorghe Hagi pulling strings.

Gullit scored first with a tap-in after a fumble by the keeper, then Van Basten made it two with another of his bullet headers. Our third came in the 38th minute, when Gullit, who received a cross on the edge of the box, calmly controlled it and had all the time in the world to fire it in. We were three ahead by half-time. Years later I would have cause to regret it when the Rossoneri reached such an unassailable position in the final. But not on this occasion. Early in the second half, Rijkaard played Van Basten in on the left to slide a shot across the keeper to make it 4–0.

We won AC Milan's first European Cup for 20 years. It had taken Sacchi nearly two seasons to shed the Mr Nobody tag but in the Camp Nou that night it was well and truly buried. Playing in a European Cup final is the highlight of any footballer's career, and for me until that moment it had been just a dream. That night showed me that dreams can come true – even my fine from Belgrade was rescinded. But could that European Cup dream come true more than once?

4
THE SECOND TIME, 1989–90

In sport it's hard to win anything once. To win it twice feels twice as hard. Why should this be? It's not really that motivation and hunger have been satisfied by victory. That is obviously a factor, but in sport you always want to win – or else why would you take part?

It's partly a question of expectation. The first time at AC Milan, we could dream of winning but could not know how it felt. Now the situation had changed and as we tried to win for the second time, we were chasing something more concrete. Not just a dream, but a reality.

But the bigger problem for Milan was more specific. The win had put a target on our back. We had established ourselves as European champions, entitling us to defend our trophy the following season. Every fresh opponent would take to the field against us, desperate to beat the holders, the champions. So they had much more fire in their bellies.

They also had more knowledge. The Sacchi style of play had been a mystery, even (or perhaps especially) for Real

Madrid. We had won partly by never letting anyone settle in possession. Italian clubs were getting used to playing against us. In fact, Inter had finished 11 points ahead of us in Serie A to win the 1988–9 Scudetto. There were still only two points given for a win in those days, so that was quite a gap. Now European opponents knew more about us too because our triumphs over Real and Steaua had been seen on TV screens all over the continent.

Those two clubs, if drawn against us, would be seeking revenge, armed with more information on how to beat us. The other big teams who had qualified included former winners such as PSV Eindhoven, Benfica and Bayern Munich. And then there were the new kids on the block. Marseille had recently been acquired by Bernard Tapie, who was just as colourful and charismatic an owner as Silvio Berlusconi, and just as eager to win the European Cup. He was very open about it, and more than willing to pay whatever it took. He had money to burn, and he spent it on some very big names. Any team that could field a strike force consisting of Jean-Pierre Papin, the English winger Chris Waddle and the great Uruguayan Enzo Francescoli, supported by a midfield containing Didier Deschamps and Jean Tigana, was going to take some beating.

If our pressing game was no longer a secret, nor were our Dutch superstars. Sacchi once made a revealing comment about the Dutch trio when asked whether the media had a tendency to place too much emphasis on Gullit, Van Basten

THE SECOND TIME, 1989–90

and Rijkaard at the expense of the rest of us. 'It wasn't just the Dutch,' Sacchi replied, 'or the squad, though they were magnificent. It was the system of play that delivered our success. The system was ultimately the leader out on the pitch; it never got injured or tired. It wasn't the players who won all those big games. It was the way we played.' This way of thinking would have a big influence on me in the early days of my own coaching career.

So now, we had to begin again. And set against the disadvantage of being a known quantity, and a big potential scalp, we gained one significant advantage. We now knew that the dream was attainable. Because we were the champions again after so long, the importance of the competition had begun to grow for us. As players we went into every game with a greater motivation than maybe we could maintain in Serie A. We felt it was our cup – it had our name on it – and we weren't going to let go of it easily.

There was no difficulty in the first round. Drawn against the Finnish champions HJK Helsinki, we had a 5–0 aggregate victory. Ours was an unfamiliar side. All our scorers were less well-known names – Stefano Borgonovo, Giovanni Stroppa, Daniele Massaro and Alberico Evani – which proved that we had a strong squad beyond our big stars. I didn't play in the first leg, while in the second, although I could never be a 'flying' winger, I was played wide on the right.

Inter were also drawn against Scandinavian opposition, but their experience shows just how slippery the early rounds of any knockout cup can be. They had won the Scudetto with a trio of great West German players to match our three Dutchmen: Lothar Matthäus, Andreas Brehme and Jürgen Klinsmann. Within the year these three would become World Cup winners. But now, playing the Swedish champions IFK Malmö, they were dumped out 2–1 on aggregate. This embarrassing defeat was masterminded by a little-known English manager named Roy Hodgson. Inter must have remembered the name and the defeat well; five years later they appointed him as their coach.

Of course, the elimination of potential rivals for the trophy worked to the advantage of all the big teams that remained in the competition. If Inter were out, it meant we wouldn't have to overcome them later. In the second round either Steaua or PSV would leave early too because they had been drawn against each other. But in terms of pitting giant versus giant, that was nothing compared to the draw we were landed with. When the names came out of the hat, AC Milan would once again have to take on Real Madrid. And this time we couldn't surprise them.

This early clash, in which the winner takes all, was exactly the type of tie that the Champions League would eventually be designed to eliminate. The thinking of men like Berlusconi was that football was entertainment. Yes, of course, there were fans in the stadium who were the primary spectators. But the entertainment was designed to reach a far larger audience on television. This was where the big money

THE SECOND TIME, 1989–90

would be made. But if Milan or Madrid – or Inter – were threatened with the Russian roulette of knockout football, that income stream could never be guaranteed. Accidents could always happen and that's not good for business.

It had happened to the then holders Liverpool when they were eliminated by Nottingham Forest in the first round in 1978–9. It had happened to Maradona and Napoli against Real Madrid in 1987–8. For Berlusconi, a draw that pitted two recent semi-finalists against each other so early indicated that the European Cup was becoming, in his words, 'a historical anachronism. It is economic nonsense that a club such as Milan might be eliminated in the first round,' he argued. 'It is not modern thinking.' He even went so far as to propose the inception of a concept he called the European Super League.

But I'm getting ahead of myself. At the time not only did I not understand that side of the game, but I also really didn't care. I was a footballer. For me the only important consideration was that, just six months after Milan had demolished Madrid 5–0 at the semi-final stage of the previous season's competition, Real were coming back to the San Siro with revenge on their minds.

It was up to us to make sure that Milan didn't join Inter and Steaua in the bin. It was a worry that we were without Gullit. He had sustained an injury to his meniscus in the previous season's semi-final and had had a quick operation that fixed the knee, temporarily, allowing him to play in the final. But when he started to train again in pre-season the knee injury flared up, which meant he would eventually miss almost the entire 1989–90 season.

But who needs three Dutchmen when two will do the job? Even without Ruud we still managed to dominate John Toshack's Madrid team and won 2–0. We were two up in no time. With only ten minutes on the clock Van Basten completely lost his marker with a sharp turn to create space on the right that enabled him to fashion a perfect cross to the centre of the goal, where Rijkaard, making a late run, nodded the ball home completely unchallenged.

Five minutes later and Rijkaard returned the favour. Madrid dwelt on the ball in the defensive third and Rijkaard won a tremendous sliding challenge that sent the ball straight into Van Basten's path. Van Basten bore down on Buyo, the Madrid keeper, only to be brought down inches *outside* the penalty area by the keeper.

The referee and linesman conferred and awarded the penalty. Interestingly, had the events taken place today, the Rijkaard challenge would probably have been ruled a foul, and VAR would have ruled the foul on Rijkaard by the goalkeeper to be outside the penalty area and the goalkeeper would have been sent off. None of that happened; Van Basten scored from the spot and that's how it remained. I admit, this was a controversial decision. The TV replay made it clear that a penalty should not have been awarded. But the result was a fair reflection of our dominance.

THE SECOND TIME, 1989–90

The return at the Bernabéu was a nasty affair. It was a physical battle from the start, and was the sort of ugly game that just couldn't happen today. Van Basten had by now established himself as so dominant, with his height and skill and mobility, that the only way other teams could think to contain him was to target him. Early on in this match he broke completely clear only to be hacked down outside the penalty area by Manuel Sanchís. This was a clear goalscoring opportunity and would be a straight red in today's game. Almost every player in a white shirt stood intimidatingly over Van Basten as he received treatment, so we too gathered round our team-mate to protect him. The next player to mistake Van Basten's leg for the ball was Fernando Hierro, who made a disgraceful knee-high tackle from behind, again leaving Marco requiring medical attention, again without a booking.

If their tactic for taking on our pressing game was to get physical, it didn't work. We caught them offside 24 times. Eventually a player of theirs was booked for kicking the ball hard at Evani as he lay prone on the grass after being hacked down. Four of our players were booked, and three of theirs. With a quarter of an hour to go Sanchís was sent off for a vicious chop from behind at Massaro's knee, and Massaro was soon in the wars again. A wonderful cross-field ball from Baresi found him in acres of space on the right, only for the Madrid keeper to hare across and shoulder-barge him into touch as if he was a linebacker bundling a wide receiver out of play in the NFL. Incredible stuff. Amazingly, there was no booking for the keeper, who trotted unapologetically back to his penalty area.

On it went. This was not the beautiful game. For the most part we completely outplayed them without managing to convert our superiority into an equaliser. They had scored on the cusp of half-time when, in a crowded area, Butragueño nodded in a ball that had bounced back up off the post. But nor could they find that second goal to match the two we'd scored at home.

And so, for the second season running we had beaten Real. No doubt the hierarchy in Madrid joined Berlusconi in his campaign to avoid such financially unfortunate outcomes in the future. At the end of the game Gullit skipped onto the pitch with a big grin looking like a top model wearing a sharp club suit and gave us all a hug, me included. We couldn't wait to welcome his strength and confidence back on the pitch in a Rossonero shirt, but we would have to. He was still injured four months later when the quarter-final came round in March.

That tie came with a heavy burden of history. Our opponents were Mechelen, who may have been Belgian champions but their ground was too small for such a big European game. The match was transferred to the Heysel Stadium in nearby Brussels. This was the first time a European club game had been played at the Belgian stadium since it was the scene of the terrible tragedy in 1985 when so many Juventus supporters had died.

THE SECOND TIME, 1989-90

Belgium was a strong footballing nation at the time. Their national side had lost to Argentina in the semi-final of the previous World Cup, and in the next one, the 1990 tournament, they were knocked out by England in the round of 16 with the last kick of extra time. Several of the Mechelen players we faced went on to play in that World Cup, including the captain, Lei Clijsters. They were ultra-cautious against us, defending deep and not trying too hard to launch attacks on our goal. So the game ended in a goalless draw.

It made for an interesting test case because this was the first time that Sacchi's high press had failed. Mechelen didn't play the ball through the midfield. Instead, their tactic was to launch long balls punted upfield by their goalkeeper, and when it came down from the skies they would fight for the second ball. It was very frustrating. We were under strict orders from Sacchi to play our usual way, but you can't press for possession when the ball is always in the air. It was an interesting lesson that I had cause to remember when I became a coach and took on high-pressing teams like Jürgen Klopp's Liverpool. If you want to beat the press and you can't go through it or round it, you go over it.

It was much the same in the second leg, but as things went on the tension rose and the atmosphere got niggly. Clijsters was sent off for cynically bringing down Donadoni as he broke for goal in the 90th minute. In extra time Donadoni soon followed him off the pitch when a defender manhandled him and he threw a retaliatory punch. Five minutes later, in the chaos that often follows a deflected free kick, Tassotti hooked the ball into Van Basten's path, and we went one up. Mechelen now had to come out and play – they'd go through if they got an away goal – but they had no answer. Instead, Marco Simone went on a wonderful dribble through the heart of their defence and calmly put the game beyond doubt.

It was a good game for Milan, not such a good one for me. Simone had come on for me when, after only 25 minutes, I hurt my knee. I knew straight away that I would not play in the semi-final, and possibly not in the final if we made it that far. So once again I found myself watching an important European Cup match in a suit. Maybe I can mark it down as practice for the many years I would spend on the bench after I retired, but it was an uncomfortable experience.

In the semi-final we faced Bayern. It wasn't the most creative line-up Bayern Munich have ever fielded, but they were very solid at the back: three of their defensive players would be on the pitch for West Germany's World Cup victory that summer in Rome. In the first game at the San Siro we managed not to concede an away goal but took our time scoring a home one. Deep into the second half they conceded a soft penalty and Van Basten did what Van Basten does. Then we went to Munich and were as dominant as ever but their keeper, Raimond Aumann, had a phenomenal night stopping shot after shot. With half an hour of the tie left, Baresi

THE SECOND TIME, 1989–90

and Costacurta both missed tackles, which must have happened almost never in their entire centre-back partnership, allowing Thomas Strunz to run through and level. Again, we were forced to endure extra time.

Salvation came after ten minutes when Maldini challenged for a half-clearance and poked the ball over the defence for Borgonovo, on as a sub, to run on to. There looked like no way through the keeper, or round him, so Borgonovo cleverly tapped a nice little lob over Aumann instead. Bayern were going to need to score against us twice more and thankfully managed it only once.

So, for the second year running, we were in the final of the European Cup. Although four clubs had won the title consecutively in the 1970s – Ajax and Bayern both three times in a row, then Liverpool and Nottingham Forest twice – the record books say that in the 1980s it was becoming harder to get to the European summit and stay there. Impossible, in fact. In the past decade no club had won it consecutively, and only Liverpool had even got to the final for a second year running. It was now 1990 and we were entering uncharted territory. Could we do what no Italian club since Inter, starring the great Sandro Mazzola, had achieved (in 1964 and '65)? Could Milan go and win it again?

The other question for me was more personal. Would I even be playing in the final in Vienna? By the time the game came round I had been out of action for two months. Fortunately – and, I think, bravely – Sacchi believed in me enough to bring me in from the cold. This was a fantastic confidence-builder for me. He often used to tell me I was important, that I was his guy on the pitch, and here was the evidence that he really meant it. He was as good as his word. From my perspective it was a new feeling to be more of a general than a foot soldier, which was definitely my role in the midfield at Roma, where there were better and more experienced players in the side than me. Now I was 30, and Sacchi gave me a lot of responsibility. Though not fully fit, Gullit was also back from his season-long lay-off.

Our opponents were Benfica, who hadn't won the competition since 1962 but were strong enough to overcome Marseille in the semi-final. Not every European Cup final can be a classic. There is so much at stake, and in 1990 there was the added shadow of the coming World Cup, which Italy would be hosting. The Dutch players may have been thinking about that, and so too my Italian team-mates. Portugal had not qualified. Indeed, between the great side starring Eusébio in 1966 and the 2002 team featuring Luís Figo and Rui Costa, they went to only one World Cup tournament. The country's record at European club level was another story. This was the third time in four years that a Portuguese club had reached the European Cup final.

There were no major stars in their side. They were composed of Portuguese and Brazilians with a big Swede up front. If anything, their best asset was on the bench in the form of their coach, Sven-Göran Eriksson. I had a lot of

THE SECOND TIME, 1989–90

inside knowledge on Sven because he had been my coach at Roma, coming in when still young as the replacement for his compatriot Nils Liedholm. I liked him. It was very sad to lose Sven in 2024. He never lost his temper, was always respectful, warm and approachable. He even gave me the honour of making me club captain for a season, albeit only after other senior players had turned down the role. But his main strength was a deep knowledge of football. He was tactically very astute and full of new ideas, while at the same time strict in enforcing a plan. I knew that he would send out a team that was well organised and would keep to a very disciplined 4–4–2 formation.

It was not a great game. In fact, it was actually pretty boring according to anyone unlucky enough to watch it. Benfica played what we might today call a low block, where the defending team retreat into their own defensive third without attempting to win the ball back after losing it further forward.

Maybe Milan were more cautious than we should have been. Our back line of Italy's finest defenders – Tassotti, Costacurta, Baresi and Maldini – kept the Benfica attack at bay relatively easily whenever they had a decent share of the possession and we always looked the most likely to score. Eventually we did, through a great back-to-front goal that was straight out of the Sacchi coaching manual. We countered a Benfica attack with just two perfect forward passes. The first pass was drilled by Costacurta to Van Basten, from

THE DREAM

back to front, and the second pass, Van Basten's first-time flick into the path of Rijkaard as he ran past him and the Benfica defenders, into the space behind their back line. Rijkaard almost casually knocked it past the onrushing Benfica keeper with the outside of his right foot before wheeling away to his left and into the congratulatory embrace of all of us. It was yet another goal fashioned in the Netherlands.

Not long after that, with 15 minutes still to go, I was substituted. Although no player likes to go off before the whistle in such a big game, to be honest it was a relief. Returning from injury, I had found the final more hard going than I expected. And the same was probably true of AC Milan across the length of the campaign. We had not been quite the force we'd been the previous season. But the end result was the same.

We were champions of Europe, again. Could we make it three in a row? A new dream.

PART TWO

LEAN YEARS

5
MR SOMEBODY, 1990–5

The short answer was no. As a farmer's son I knew all too well the concept of lean years. These are the years that you must endure, from which you must emerge stronger if you want to enjoy the fertile years.

AC Milan had won a Scudetto and back-to-back European Cups in three consecutive seasons. Not a bad return for Mr Nobody. But the Rossoneri's shooting star eventually had to fall and the descent began in the 1990–1 season.

I don't know whether disappointment at that summer's World Cup had anything to do with it, or whether it was simply mental and physical exhaustion. The Netherlands did not have a happy tournament, struggling out of their group and into an intense round of 16 clash at the San Siro with West Germany that was almost like a local derby between the stars of Milan and Inter. Rijkaard and German centre-forward Rudi Völler were sent off together in the first half. Italy made it to the semi-finals, dragged there by the heroics of the Sicilian striker Totò Schillaci. But maybe the pressure of hosting the tournament got to us. We lost to Maradona's Argentina. I had a difficult tournament myself, getting injured in the first group game, which limited my involvement to three matches. One was the third-place play-off against England.

When Milan reassembled for the 1990–1 season, as in the previous season we won both the European Super Cup and the Intercontinental Cup. They were both nice additions to the trophy room, but only the European Cup really mattered. We had a bye in the first round after the bad behaviour of the Ajax fans had earned them a ban from the competition. In the next round we struggled past Club Brugge on a 1–0 aggregate. Then came our first encounter with Olympique de Marseille. This was the type of big game that both our president Silvio Berlusconi and theirs, Bernard Tapie, hankered for. In fact, it ended in farce, with disastrous consequences for Milan.

The first leg at the San Siro was drawn 1–1 and we knew we had a mountain to climb when we faced them at their place. We were losing 1–0 to a spectacular cross-box volley on 75 minutes from Chris Waddle, and we were staring elimination in the face. Waddle had just gone on a wonder dribble from their half deep into the box when the referee's whistle was mistaken for full-time. Assuming the game was over we started to exchange shirts. But the referee clarified that there were still three minutes remaining. Just as he ordered us to resume the game, one of the floodlights failed and the whole stadium descended into semi-gloom. Chaos reigned as match officials and coaching staff swarmed onto the pitch, followed by photographers eager to capture it all, as everyone tried to establish what on earth would happen next.

It took 20 minutes for the lighting to be restored. By then our general manager, Galliani, had lost patience and ordered us to abandon the game. Perhaps he was remembering the precedent from when we had had to replay the leg in Belgrade that was abandoned before the finish. Could he have been hoping for a rematch? Our club lawyer as well as our captain Baresi tried to reason with him, but Galliani would not be overruled. So off we trudged. The match was abandoned, and by way of punishment UEFA decided to award Marseille a couple of extra goals. So the record books state that we lost 4–1, even though there is no name on the scoresheet next to those two phantom goals. Elimination was a bitter enough pill to swallow, but worse was the year-long ban from the competition that Galliani's protest had incurred.

It turned out that that game was particularly poignant for me. That was my last night of European football. I never played in the competition again. It was a strange and unsatisfactory way to end my time as a European Cup footballer and it was also the beginning of the end for one of the greatest club sides in the cup's history. The European reign of Arrigo Sacchi's Immortals was over. Perhaps it would have

THE DREAM

sweetened the pill if we had won the Scudetto that year, but we finished well behind Sampdoria.

Sadly, at a certain stage there was a breakdown in trust between Sacchi and some of his players. Most damaging was the rift with Marco van Basten. To be honest, Sacchi had always had a complicated relationship with his star players. It's difficult to put a finger on why exactly, but it may have had something to do with the fact that he had never played at a high level. It's not as if he didn't love and admire his players. He even singled out the stars, especially Gullit, and stressed their importance to the team, acknowledging that without great players the system he favoured would not work as well as it did. The clash, such as it was, had to do with that system. For Sacchi, the highly regimented system – the 4–4–2 formation with a high press that created attacking opportunities – was the ultimate star of AC Milan. Everything and everyone were in the service of the system.

He expected even the likes of Van Basten and Gullit to fit into the specific and organised system the way the rest of us did. Perhaps that fed an idea in the minds of some that they were undervalued. Football is a sport where the collective intelligence of the players, and their effort as a team, is of equal importance to their individual skills. At the same time, while tactics are clearly important, they should never be allowed to smother a player's natural abilities and creative instincts. To execute tactics at the highest level, players have to make instant on-field decisions. In Sacchi's eyes the players and the system were totally interdependent. One could not exist without the other, and vice versa. That is the reality, irrespective of what coaches may like to think. My method, however, is to listen when decisions are not clear, when there is uncertainty. I listen to others; to the players, the coaches, to anybody who might help. In that way the players, especially, are engaged with the final decision and are, therefore, responsible for it on the pitch.

Berlusconi loved Sacchi, so rather than sacking the coach who had delivered his dream of European dominance, the president pulled some strings and arranged for him to be appointed as the new coach of the Italian national team. Sacchi took up that role in 1991 and it was under him that I won the last of my 26 caps.

At the same time my club career was drawing to a close. Sacchi was replaced by Fabio Capello. This was seen at the time as a controversial choice because he was an inside man with no great track record to merit such a promotion. He certainly had a track record by the end of the season. The lack of European football in 1991–2 meant at least that we could concentrate on domestic football, and we won the Scudetto by a mile without losing a single game. It was an astonishing achievement, never before done in Serie A and matched only once since, when Juventus did the same 20 years later. In fact, Capello brought home three Scudetti in a row and, in 1994, resumed the club's tradition of European dominance by winning its first Champions League.

THE DREAM

I was around for only the first of his titles, although thanks to persistent problems with my knee I wasn't significantly involved and my place at the heart of the midfield was taken by Demetrio Albertini. In my very last game for Milan, I came off the bench with 20 minutes to go. This was a nice gesture by Capello that allowed me to say goodbye to the fans and them to do the same to me. We were already two up against Hellas Verona thanks to Van Basten and Gullit. But then something incredible happened. I scored two goals in two minutes – and they weren't bad ones either. Rijkaard teed me up to drive a shot home from outside the box. Then a minute later I caught a defender in possession, snuck into the box and tapped the ball past the keeper. There was nothing wrong with my 33-year-old knees for my last ever day out on the pitch. It was a fairytale finish to a career that had brought me more than I could ever have imagined when I started out with the simple dream of becoming a footballer. Above all stood those two European Cups.

The question of what to do next was solved by an invitation from Sacchi. He asked me to join him as an assistant coach with the national squad. I suppose it made sense to him. He had often spoken of me as his representative on the pitch, and I thought of myself as a student of his, so we both knew that we thought along the same lines. It was the only way to keep my passion alive, because football is my passion, so it was just another way to love football and follow new dreams.

MR SOMEBODY, 1990-5

Therefore, my coaching career started at the pinnacle of the game, with the Azzurri. Our task for the next two years was to qualify for the 1994 FIFA World Cup, which was being hosted in the United States. This we did in a tightly contested group that also included Switzerland, who qualified with us, Portugal and Scotland. And so I found myself acting as assistant coach in a squad for the World Cup finals that included no fewer than eight of my old Rossoneri teammates. On top of that, I had played with other internationals at the previous World Cup. The strange thing is I don't remember my inclusion in the coaching set-up creating any difficulties. Perhaps it was useful for Sacchi to have someone who knew the players at a different level to him; someone who could act as a buffer and a conduit.

The tournament went incredibly well but not well enough. Led from the front by Roberto Baggio, Italy got all the way to the final, which was held in Pasadena, California. The game against Brazil was extremely tense and produced no goals after two hours. And so, for the third time in my career – after the 1984 European Cup final and the tense three-match tie against Red Star Belgrade in 1989 – I found myself nervously watching from beyond the touchline as the intense drama of a penalty shoot-out unfurled on the pitch. We didn't have our shooting boots on that day. I remember thinking that it was surely impossible for Baresi and Baggio, the two great titans of the side, to take aim and miss the target. It turned out I was wrong. Somewhere in California they're still looking for the ball that my old club captain whacked over the bar. If that moment taught me anything, it is that football is played in the mind as well as with the feet. It was an important lesson that I would take with me into my coaching career.

Why does anyone become a coach? In my case there is no easy explanation. It was never my ambition to spend the next 30 years in the dugout. I have always thought of myself as a player first and foremost, who just happened to become a coach. But the invitation to join Sacchi and the Azzurri suggested that he could see something in me. He knew a thing or two, but not even he could have guessed that I would go on to be so lucky and enjoy so much success over so many years.

At the end of the 1994–5 season I received an offer to go back to my hometown club at Reggiana. It came at the right moment because I felt that it was time for me to strike out on my own. I had learned a lot with Sacchi and when I told him about the job offer, he agreed and wished me luck. I knew that I would need it and that it would be a steep learning curve. I didn't appreciate how steep.

The approach had a romantic element to it because I was a local boy. My birthplace in Reggiolo is only 25 kilometres north of Reggio Emilia, where Reggiana play. But it was pragmatic of the club to think of me too. They had just been relegated to Serie B and they needed to cheer up the fans with an eye-catching appointment. My name seemed to fit the bill. In that way I was definitely different from Sacchi,

MR SOMEBODY, 1990–5

who was known as Signor Nessuno or Mr Nobody. As a former international who had been on the pitch for Milan's recent triumphs, I guess they saw me as a Signor Qualcuno: a Mr Somebody.

I hadn't got my coaching qualifications yet and so I had to hire someone who did have them to satisfy the league's regulations. I brought Giorgio Ciaschini, a licensed goalie coach, on board. My lack of training as a coach soon showed. My memory of being a player was so recent that it was difficult for me to be the boss who speaks to the squad and expects them to listen. We were bottom of the table after seven games with zero points and I'm sure it was only my name that saved me from the sack before we managed to turn things around and win our eighth game. Eventually we got our act together and finished fourth, winning promotion to Serie A. It was a small success, but it moved me very slightly forward towards my first contact with the Champions League as a coach.

What I started to learn in that first season is that my connection with the players, which comes from a memory of having been one, is my greatest strength, and yet it can also be a weakness. The strength is that I will always try to understand the players' position. The weakness is that sometimes it can affect the needs of the club. It can dilute the focus on what the club needs and what the team needs to do to achieve that. And that may be to the detriment of some players. As in life, balance is everything.

THE DREAM

As I started out on my coaching journey, I was determined that I would listen to everyone and anyone. I would not be afraid to learn from any source. I took a little bit from each of the coaches I had played for. From Nils Liedholm I learned to have a sense of humour about things. Sven-Göran Eriksson was also a reference point and an inspiration, and I have always tried to be as good as he was at managing players and never losing his temper. As for Sacchi, having watched him closely for four years at Milan and two more with the Azzurri, he was my mentor but not, in the end, my model. That had to be me: I had to create my own model. As I transitioned from playing to coaching in that first club job, I started to realise the limitations of sticking to a single philosophy. So, rather than simply copy the tactical system that had brought Sacchi so much success, I would eventually find the courage to go my own way. I understood that the biggest lesson I could take from Sacchi was not to be a Sacchi clone but an original Ancelotti.

Eventually I would learn that a coach can do only so much. You study and think and discuss and you come up with a model of playing. Then you convince the players that that way is the one that will get them through the game. You say that all your experience tells you *this* is the best way to beat this particular opposition. You persuade the players, and you drill them and you tell them your idea so many times that they hear you when they go to sleep. Then on the day of the game, you stand on the touchline and hope to God that it works.

Back in 1995, I had all this to find out.

6
A LEAGUE OF ITS OWN, 1995–2001

I would make my name in the Champions League as a manager just as I had as a player: with AC Milan. But even before I returned to the club, its owner was already casting a long shadow over my future. It was Silvio Berlusconi, the owner of AC Milan and a big figure in Italian broadcasting, who was instrumental in changing the shape and format of Europe's premier competition. Obviously, he later became known for other things – he was prime minister of Italy three times and got implicated in all sorts of scandal. But in the early 1990s he was one of the architects of the Champions League.

Berlusconi's reasoning was simple. The big clubs weren't making enough money from the European Cup. If they performed badly or got unlucky in the first round, they could be eliminated after two games before the end of October. The new model, proposed at an Extraordinary UEFA Congress in Montreux in 1991, was to introduce a mini-league. Every club that qualified for it would play a minimum of six games.

THE DREAM

This meant a guarantee of more gate receipts, and more television money. The further a club went in the competition, the more lucrative it became. Once they got through the initial round there would be another mini-league before the semi-finals. With not only league champions taking part but clubs that had finished the previous season in second, third or fourth (and now even fifth) place being invited to participate, the newly named Champions League suddenly became a more attractive commercial proposition.

To a certain extent this earthquake passed me by, because I was busy assisting Sacchi with the national team. However, when I did get my first taste of the new-look competition, I didn't have much joy with it. Having started out at Reggiana in 1995, I had done well enough in that first season to get offered a job with Parma. We had a good squad full of young players who would become great stars of the game over many years. Some would go on to win the World Cup. Lilian Thuram did it with France in 1998, Fabio Cannavaro and Gigi Buffon with Italy in 2006. Buffon eventually represented his country 176 times for over 20 years. An incredible record. When I inherited him, he was just 17. Then there was Hernán Crespo. Before I signed him, he had just scored a hatful of goals for Argentina at the Olympics in Atlanta. When Parma eventually sold him, he became the most expensive player in transfer history. But in 1996 these players were all young and inexperienced. In coaching terms, so was I. Perhaps that's why it worked. We learned together.

A LEAGUE OF ITS OWN, 1995–2001

In my first season in charge, Parma finished second in Serie A behind Juventus. It was the club's highest ever position and it meant that for the first time we would go into the Champions League. It was in the Champions League group stage during that second season that I learned another important lesson. When you're playing in a mini-league, unlike in knockout football, it is not enough to avoid defeat, you must actually win games to accumulate as many points as possible, as early as you can. We did manage to beat Borussia Dortmund, who won the group, but drew too many of the other games. Some of the second-placed teams went through to the next round, but only if they had the points. Juventus had 12 and went all the way to the final. We had nine and were dumped out.

The lesson I took from my first exposure to the Champions League was not to be too cautious. And this led to a second lesson, which is that you have to get as far as you can in European competition if you're not going well in the domestic league, or else there will be consequences. In Italian we say that you must 'pay the bill', *prima o poi devi pagare il conto*. In other words, the present may seem great, everything can be going well, but there is always a cost for success and the price that must be paid awaits you in the future.

I had paid my first bill with that job.

I paid it at my next job too. When I look back now, it doesn't quite make sense that I ended up in charge at Juventus. I had been a player at clubs that were among their

THE DREAM

biggest rivals. Personally, I didn't really warm to the city of Turin. It felt gloomy to me. I was in the middle of negotiating with Fenerbahçe in Turkey when the invitation came to go and meet the top brass at Juve. The agreement we soon reached was that I would take charge at the start of the 1999–2000 season. I signed the contract on the autostrada halfway between Turin and Milan – proper old-school cloak-and-dagger stuff. Some of my friends thought I had taken leave of my senses. So did the Juventus fans. There was no love lost for me in that quarter. I can still remember the day I was introduced to some representatives of the supporters' trust, having taken up my post earlier than expected when Marcello Lippi was sacked mid-season.

'I know that you're not happy about it,' the general manager Luciano Moggi said to them, 'but this is the manager, and I don't care if you support or you don't support him, we will support him 100 per cent.'

'We don't care,' they replied. 'We don't like him, and we are going to fight him every step of the way.'

I had to sit there and listen to this nonsense. To be fair, the fans were as good as their word. They really didn't like me. Arriving at my first game in charge, which was away to Piacenza, I spotted that the travelling supporters, who are always the most fanatical, had created a banner. 'A pig can't coach,' it said. 'Ancelotti leave.' Later, when I took the team to the San Siro, the Milan fans applauded my arrival on the touchline while the Juventus fans whistled.

A LEAGUE OF ITS OWN, 1995–2001

The only way to get them on my side, or at least keep them quiet, was to win everything in sight. Juventus had won the European Cup in 1985 on that terrible day in the Heysel Stadium in Brussels when a collapsed wall killed 39 people, mostly Juventus fans. They won the Champions League 11 years later with a team led by my old international teammate Gianluca Vialli. By the time I arrived, the star of the team was Zinedine Zidane. He and I would go on to share a lot of history, but his first job was to teach me another vital lesson that would stand me in good stead for the rest of my career: flexibility.

I'm a big fan of 4–4–2. Always have been, always will be. For me it's the most logical and structured way of setting up ten outfield players on a football pitch, which is, after all, rectangular. But it does have its limitations and challenges. It can be more comfortable to pass laterally with 4–4–2 than vertically, which can make players lazy and encourage crab-like movements with the ball. In making a priority of defence it ensures that games might be harder to lose but that might also make them harder to win. The problem is that some players don't quite fit into such a system.

At the start of my career, when I was less sure of myself, I found it difficult to think outside the box. I lost the chance to work with two great Italian number 10s for that reason. Gianfranco Zola left Parma for Chelsea soon after I took charge because I couldn't coalesce his way of playing and mine. If I'd been more flexible, it's very possible he would

THE DREAM

have stayed. And I made a mistake by missing the opportunity to buy Roberto Baggio, a brilliant footballer who I knew well from my time with the Italian national team, both as a player in the 1990 World Cup and as assistant coach in 1994. The problem for me as a coach with a fixed idea about formations was that he didn't fit into the pattern of how I set up my team. So, I resisted buying him.

I wasn't going to make a trio of mistakes with Zidane. He was just too good at what he did to be constrained by a system. He was a player of pure talent. By that I mean that he had a body that should not have been so balletic, so smooth, so elegant and at the same time so powerful, so quick and so athletic. How could I play such a majestic talent wide on the left or the right in a 4–4–2? I had to find a way of moulding my thinking around the unique abilities of a consummate playmaker. So I decided for the first time to make do with a three-man defence, set up four midfielders in front of them and then sat Zidane behind a pair of strikers.

And it seemed to work in Serie A. I joined the club in February 1999 and we didn't lose a game until just before the semi-final of the Champions League, when we somehow managed to lose to bottom-of-the-league Empoli. Maybe our minds were thinking of the semi-final against Alex Ferguson's Manchester United. We went to Old Trafford and dominated the match but came away with only a draw. At least we had the away goal. Back in Turin we went quickly ahead with two goals from Pippo Inzaghi, a fantastic natural goalscorer whom I greatly admired – and who will be turning up again in my Champions League story. But Roy Keane was on fire that day and got a goal back with a leaping near-post header from a corner. Then he got booked, meaning he would miss the final if United got through. That only seemed to motivate him and his team-mates even more. By half-time they were level, and therefore effectively in front thanks to the away goals rule. Then they got another.

This wasn't the last time three comeback goals from an English team would spoil my night. Sometimes you just have to accept that it's not your destiny to win, and that someone up there is cheering for the opposition. This was one of the greatest nights in Manchester United's history, putting them back in the final for the first time since the era of Best, Law and Charlton. It was also important for my good friend Alex Ferguson, even if for me it was one to forget.

When I think back to my time in Turin, I realise that my business head had ruled my heart. This was another valuable lesson. As a club Juventus felt like it was run as a business. When you arrived for training, it was as if you were clocking in for a shift at the Fiat factory. I can't complain about the players. They gave me everything I asked for. Unfortunately, it was not enough. I was not enough. The following season, 2000–01, Juventus finished second for the second consecutive year. That guaranteed qualification in the Champions League, but this was only the minimum requirement. In that same season, the only full one I had at

THE DREAM

the club, we were drawn in a group that on paper did not look particularly challenging but somehow, after six games against Deportivo La Coruña, Panathinaikos and Hamburg, we managed to finish bottom.

I had been hired to bring home the Champions League. After that failure there was no future for me at Juve. The club's president Gianni Agnelli reflected that 'it is difficult to work in a city where the great part of the fans and the press are against you'. The fact is that he and all the board knew this before they hired me, but they took the risk anyway – and so did I.

When I left Juventus, I resolved to work next at a club that had a greater sense of belonging. So when Calisto Tanzi, the major shareholder of the corporation Parmalat, which almost wholly owned Parma, started wooing me to return, the idea felt like an attractive option. From the outside it might have seemed a backward step, but after Turin my old job looked like a safe haven. I was on my way to sign on the dotted line, but then the phone rang, and everything changed.

My football family was calling me back home.

PART THREE

MILAN
THE COACHING YEARS

7
CHRISTMAS COMES EARLY, 2001–2

I had been away from AC Milan for nine seasons. In the years I was away the club was managed by Fabio Capello, who stayed on until 1996, Arrigo Sacchi, who came back for a season, and Capello again, returning for the 1997–8 season. Alberto Zaccheroni won the Scudetto in 1999 but the following season he was fired when he failed to get to the Champions League final, which was to be held at the San Siro. Four replacements rapidly came and went, including Cesare Maldini, Paolo's dad, and my old team-mate Mauro Tassotti. My predecessor presided over a bad start to the 2000–1 season and Berlusconi grew impatient. The final straw was a 1–0 defeat at Torino.

It so happened that the club's vice president Adriano Galliani and I had spoken a few days earlier about something completely different, but during the conversation I let him know that I was about to go back to Parma. Mentioning this was not a calculated move on my part, it was just social chit-chat. But Galliani acted swiftly, speaking to Berlusconi, who

THE DREAM

sacked the incumbent coach and crossed his fingers that I hadn't already signed on the dotted line at Parma. I hadn't, but I was going to the following day. In fact, I was already on my way to the club when I got a call from Galliani.

'I'm going to your house,' he said.

'Why?' I replied.

'I spoke with Berlusconi, and we agree that you have to come here, to Milan. We are ready for you.'

I turned off my phone, did a U-turn and drove home to sign for Milan, then turned the phone back on to call Tanzi at Parma, whose hand I had shaken only days before.

'Sorry,' I said to him, 'but Milan is my family. I hope that you can understand.' He wasn't happy. Nor were the Parma fans. But there are times in football when you can put too much stress on loyalty, often without it being reciprocated. It rarely seems to work both ways. I just could not turn down the opportunity that had suddenly presented itself.

The minute I arrived at Milanello, the club's training ground, I felt back at home. Perhaps it helped that the squad contained a quartet of survivors from my last season as a player all the way back in 1992. Paolo Maldini, at 33, was now the same age as I had been when I decided to retire, but, unlike me, his body showed no sign of fatigue or wear and tear. Billy Costacurta was 35 and yet played more than 30 games that first season. Demetrio Albertini and Marco Simone were still Rossoneri too. That's quite a testament to what I mean about the club being a family. Once they joined, the Italian players did not want to leave. After retirement the likes of Baresi and Evani stayed on, and Tassotti became my assistant. And it wasn't just the players. Even the kitman and the waiters in the restaurant had been there for a very long time.

In making the transition from Milan player to Milan coach, I had help from Maldini. When I arrived, I found myself looking at him as if he were still my team-mate. But as the leader of the playing group, he made it clear that we had to have a professional relationship, that it was appropriate for him to treat me as the boss now. There should be a gap. I understood, and I was grateful to him. I also had help from him out on the pitch. He was the ideal captain, who had the personality and the ability to lead from the front. He was a strong character, who never showed fear or worry and drove his team-mates along through positive encouragement.

The squad was much more of a melting pot than it had been when I left. Back then, apart from the Dutch, we were all Italians. Now I inherited players from all over Europe, South America and Africa. The most high-profile of them were Andriy Shevchenko from Ukraine, the Georgian Kakha Kaladze, Rui Costa from Portugal and the Brazilians Serginho and Roque Júnior. The squad still pumped with Italian blood, and I would come to rely on three players in particular. In midfield there was Andrea Pirlo, who at 22 was just finding his feet, and the tireless Gennaro Gattuso. And up front there was Pippo Inzaghi, whom I already knew well from our time together at Juventus.

But it became clear to me in my first months there that, despite the presence of all these stars, the squad needed improving. Berlusconi had spent a lot of money on Inzaghi, Rui Costa and Pirlo. It was my job to persuade him to spend some more at the end of my first season. The three great Dutchmen had long since departed, but we signed another one in the shape of Clarence Seedorf, a central midfielder who was as powerful as he was skilful. I managed to get both him and the Croatian defender Dario Šimić from Inter.

Seedorf was an interesting player to manage. He was strong, but he could also be headstrong. While I had some experience of the Dutch mentality, Seedorf was on another level. When he arrived, he was always arguing with his teammates, as if he imagined himself to be in charge. This was really just a sign of his passion, but it could come out a little too forcefully. 'You are not the manager,' the players told him. 'You don't have to talk like this.' I realised it was best to channel his instinct by giving him certain tasks. If I told him to take on a particular responsibility on the pitch, he would do it. But I also suggested he be more polite if he wanted to be listened to. We got there soon enough, and he became an integral leader of the midfield. He is one of the great players I was lucky enough to coach, a beast with finesse to match.

Just as importantly, the hole long since left by Baresi still needed filling. I argued that we had to splash the cash to get the best quality, and recommended we buy Alessandro Nesta, who had been a mainstay of the Lazio and Italy defence for several

CHRISTMAS COMES EARLY, 2001–2

seasons. In fact, I mentioned the idea to Nesta himself long before anyone else heard about it. This came about because several months earlier the national squad had been training at Milanello, and I took the opportunity to have a quiet word.

'Next season,' I told him, 'you have to come here.'

'No, no, no,' he replied. "I want to stay at Lazio because you know I am a Lazio fan. Also, I don't like Milan. I prefer Rome.'

Berlusconi, whose company was going through some financial difficulties, was anxious about spending €30 million on a defender. He preferred his money to go on the glamour players who did their showy work at the other end of the pitch. But it doesn't matter how many goals you score: if you let more in you get nowhere. I decided to use a similar arm-twisting tactic on him that Sacchi had used when persuading the club to buy me from Roma 15 years earlier. 'President,' I told him, 'Everyone wants to win the Champions League, but if you don't buy Nesta, we won't win it. Give me Nesta and I will give you the Champions League.' That did the trick, and Nesta came at the end of that season.

When he arrived, I started to impress upon him the increased demands that would be laid upon him now that he was at a bigger club. Every game was vital, not just the Rome derby. And I told him to follow the example of his new team-mates. 'If you want to be the best then you have to follow the best,' I said to him. 'Watch and learn from Maldini, from Costacurta – from all the Milan professionals. If you follow them, you will understand what to do.'

THE DREAM

Of course, you can't win the Champions League unless you qualify for it. We started to improve across that first season and managed to squeak up into fourth place. But this by no means guaranteed an autumn of lucrative European action. Before our name went into the hat for the group games, first we had to take part in one of those tricky two-legged preliminary ties in August. We were drawn against the Czech side Slovan Liberec and managed to survive by the skin of our teeth.

I went for a relatively defensive selection for the home leg, a traditional 4–4–2 with Rui Costa at the sharp end of a flattish diamond shape, because I worried about the havoc that an away goal could cause us when we were still learning to work as a team with new recruits. So a clean sheet was my priority.

We got an early scare when a shot of theirs bounced back off the post into the arms of our keeper, Dida. But we did manage to go into the second leg with a goal advantage when Inzaghi scored one of his typical poacher's goals. Then we got a serious wake-up call in the away game. I had noticed that something was wrong with our mentality before the game. The strange experience of playing such an unlikely tie in a small town north of Prague so early in the season seemed to unsettle the players. I remember how in training the day before the game they got frustrated that they were not able to string any passes together.

Clearly, they were agitated, so that night before dinner I called a meeting and told them to calm down. Tomorrow would be fine. It seemed to work because in the first half we doubled our lead and got the crucial away goal when Inzaghi scored from a clever Rui Costa pass. But then we let them score twice as well. Maldini lost his footing in the box and let them steal the first goal. Then they got another in the 88th minute. Even though the scorer was then sent off for a second yellow card, we still suffered like beasts in those final minutes as they just kept coming at us. A little team with no major stars had come very close to ruining my relationship with the Champions League as coach of AC Milan before it had even begun. Slovan Liberec taught me a valuable lesson: in knock-out games, never, ever underestimate the opposition. Play against the 11 men in front of you, not the reputation of the team nor the size of the club or the country.

That said, it is worth analysing the particular circumstances of the tie. Sometimes teams can be rusty after the close season, and not quite ready for such an important pair of matches before Serie A has even got going. Was that an excuse for us? It's more likely that all the Italian players in the squad were still hung over from the disappointment of that summer's World Cup hosted by Japan and South Korea. Maldini was the captain of the Italian team, which was very surprisingly eliminated by the South Koreans in the round of 16. Italy conceded a last-minute equaliser just before full-time and then came the sucker punch of a golden goal scored in extra time. It was quite a public trauma. Maldini retired from international football straight afterwards.

THE DREAM

Having progressed to the group stage we now found ourselves having to face Bayern Munich, Deportivo La Coruña and Lens. Luckily for me I now had a strong squad and a lot of players to choose from. But that created its own problem. I knew that the president wanted to change the style of the team. Capello's teams were really well organised, but maybe they didn't play the way that Berlusconi appreciated. The brief was to win with more style – something you often hear from owners. He wanted not just results, but entertainment. And since he owned AC Milan, it took me no time to understand that my job, as far as Berlusconi was concerned, was to please Berlusconi. At Juventus it had been just to win, whatever the cost. Over time I came to accept that the president's whim was my command. If he wanted to come into the dressing room to tell us his jokes or even listen to the team talk, then I had to understand that it was his dressing room.

To assist with the project of playing attractive football, that summer the club signed one of the stars of the World Cup on a free transfer. Rivaldo had scored five goals, bettered only by his team-mate Ronaldo, who got eight. Together they won the tournament, beating Germany in the final. Naturally both he and the president expected him to play. As we embarked on our Champions League campaign proper, I had a headache. A good headache, but still a headache. I had to find a place in my midfield for Gattuso, Rui Costa, Pirlo, Seedorf and other good players. Then up front I had Inzaghi, Shevchenko and the tall Dane Jon Dahl Tomasson.

CHRISTMAS COMES EARLY, 2001–2

Somehow on this chessboard there needed to be a square made open for Rivaldo.

Of course, I was very happy to see him arrive. It is obviously much better to have a player like him than not. The challenge was to keep all the players happy as individuals while also thinking about developing them into a team. The advantage of having a lot of outstanding players was that we had no need to risk anybody's fitness. 'You will get games,' I was able to reassure them. 'Things will happen with form, injuries, suspensions, and you will all get a chance.' The atmosphere was good, which is incredibly important, and as part of a fantastic squad at a great club, the players became more willing to accept that they wouldn't feature in every minute of every match. But some were easier to convince than others.

The World Cup final had been on 30 June. The contact with the Champions League came with the first leg against Slovan Liberec on 14 August. Rivaldo hadn't had a full pre-season or preparation for the match, so he didn't play. Two weeks later he was ready to make his debut as a substitute. But then at the start of the domestic season in mid-September we had a game away to Modena and I had to tell him that I was keeping him on the bench. This clearly came as a bit of a shock.

'Rivaldo has never been on the bench,' he explained.

'OK,' I told him, 'there's always a first time, and now is the right time to be the first one.'

'No, no,' he said. 'Rivaldo doesn't go on the bench.'

I was the boss, and I had to remind him of this.

THE DREAM

'Rivaldo, you have to go on the bench,' I said.

The message didn't seem to go in. He just got up and went home.

Of course, I understood him, up to a point. It is difficult for truly special players to understand why they cannot play, even when they are only 80 per cent fit. Part of their greatness is that they want to play every game, fit or injured, because they are hungry to win games and fundamentally believe that they are equipped to make a difference. This is part of what makes up a champion's personality. And yet this was a new situation for someone like me, who had been brought up to be deferential to the coach. Rivaldo clearly did not understand our relationship as I did. Maybe something in the game was changing and I was the one who didn't understand.

For my entire playing career there was a culture of deference towards the coach. The man who first picked me to play for the Azzurri in 1981 was Enzo Bearzot. He was a disciplinarian, and it is impossible to picture any player ever daring to question him. Of course, in my playing days we were sometimes encouraged to share our opinions . . . sometimes. Take the example of Falcão arriving at Roma from Brazil and questioning why we did so little training with the ball. That felt like a productive contribution. But we were now in a different era. Football had become a truly global sport. Every game was on a television channel somewhere or other and, no matter where they were from, the best players in the world were all starting to cluster together at a small group of the very top superclubs. At the same time the financial rewards for players were starting to go stratospheric. I won't say that the fundamental character of footballers changed, but they were subject to greater pressures and more public exposure, and it had some unexpected consequences – Rivaldo going home disgruntled when told he was on the bench, for example.

As the season developed, it didn't help that he was going through a difficult time in his personal life. He had left his children behind at home in Brazil, so his emotional focus was split between there and Milan. That can't have helped. But before that first game the club spoke to him and to his agent, and he came back and sat on the bench for the match against Modena. Only then did I speak with him again.

'Listen,' I said, 'it's for you, not for us. You don't have to be worried because it can happen today, it can happen in the next game, and it can happen to any player. We have a lot of games, and it means you can be more fresh when you play in the next match.'

My search for a solution intensified. Even at Juventus I had not had such a wealth of talent to choose from. What became clear to me was that it was a puzzle I couldn't solve on my own. I had to be open-minded and involve the players too. I needed their help in finding a system that allowed them to combine into a winning unit. That was the overriding priority.

Even more than at Juventus, when I had to think creatively to accommodate the genius of Zidane, I now started to relax my faith in 4–4–2. As the season progressed, and different solutions were put into practice and tested, it was the players who began to converge on a version of a system known as the Christmas Tree formation (not that this term was ever used). It was more of a stunted tree, with four at the back, three in midfield, one in the hole and two up front. As I experimented it became apparent that the best partner up front for Inzaghi was Shevchenko. Perhaps he was less of a master with the ball at his feet than Rivaldo, but his incredible pace, power and mobility gave us more of an option at the point of attack, more of a threat than with Rivaldo.

So I'm afraid it wasn't good news for the player in our squad who (along with Roque Júnior) had just won a World Cup. While he was trying to adjust to Serie A he was not playing as much as he thought he should. Part of the problem, for him but not for me, was that my solution of preferring Inzaghi and Shevchenko brought instant rewards. The pair were scoring regularly. And Tomasson was a perfect back-up, happy to be an apprentice in such a team. Meanwhile in midfield it was impossible to leave out either of Seedorf and Pirlo, and, especially, Rui Costa. Our Portuguese midfielder had blossomed after a difficult start and become very important to us. Having shown us all how good he was, it would have been a mistake on my part – or anyone else's – to think that Rui Costa would no longer be an automatic first choice. As we started out on our European campaign, for everyone except for Rivaldo, Christmas had come early.

8

THE THIRD TIME, 2002–3

If the Christmas tree was the result of an accident, it was a beautiful accident. We were up against Deportivo La Coruña in the group stage of the Champions League. Andriy Shevchenko had picked up an injury, so I had to think of a way of doing without him. Our opponents played with two deep-lying midfielders, and I calculated that without Shevchenko's mobility we would not be able to defensively cover the position of these players. They would be too deep for us to have any impact on them.

So I had to think of a solution. I decided to play two offensive midfielders who could push up on them when we didn't have the ball. You could argue that the whole idea was, in fact, born of thinking not offensively, but defensively. *How could we stop the opposition?* was uppermost in my thoughts. Typically Italian!

But behind those two I moved Andrea Pirlo back to a deeper role, as a playmaker who was almost like a quarterback. At the time Pirlo was thought of by everyone, including

THE DREAM

himself, as an attacking midfielder. But he had in fact been tested in this withdrawn role before. It was when he was a young player at Inter, who sent him out on loan to Brescia for a season. Their coach had decided that playing just behind the attackers was a waste of his ability to read the pitch and then to take advantage of it with his huge range of passing skills. There was the added issue that he was relatively slight and could be more easily knocked off the ball the further up the field he went. So, for ten games, he sat in front of the back four and, despite his initial confusion, discovered that he could be effective in this new role. The credit for this brainwave must go to the Brescia coach Carlo Mazzone.

As I was coaching Juventus at the time, I'm not quite sure how I managed to forget about this experiment. In my second season there we played host to Brescia and drew 1–1. Their goal came via Pirlo's exquisite chip from the halfway line. It landed on the right foot of Roberto Baggio, who watched the ball's approach over his shoulder and in one brilliant touch hooked it deftly round the advancing keeper before tickling it in with his left foot. Maybe it was Baggio's dazzling skill that had dimmed the memory of the kid who fired that incredible pass. It was an amazing goal.

So, one day Pirlo came up to me and suggested I stick him at the base of the midfield. Maybe my surprise was to do with his personality. We all thought of him as quite a shy man, and a bit of a loner. And yet he had an inner strength and a quiet confidence. He understood the player–coach dynamic but was never cowed by it. Technically, I had my own preconceptions to overcome. I had thought of him as someone who ran with the ball. And I worried – and so did he – that he was not a naturally defensive player, and so the duties that come with playing in that section of the pitch might be too much for him. My confidence in his ability to command the game – and deliver laser-accurate long balls for Shevchenko to chase – grew just as he grew into the role. In terms of his defensive duties, I told him that I only needed him to be in the right position. I reassured him, 'You don't have to press, you don't have to tackle, but you must track and be goal-side when it is necessary. Just be between the ball and the goal, between your man and our goal.'

So I overrode my own doubts, and history has been my judge. It was playing in that position that Pirlo won his 116 caps for the Azzurri, as well as the man of the match award when Italy lifted the World Cup in 2006.

The new formation worked. We beat Lens 2–1 at home, Inzaghi scoring twice in four minutes. Then we beat Deportivo 4–0 away. Gattuso and Seedorf, who opened the scoring with a pile-driver, gave us all the energy and muscle we needed in front of Pirlo. Meanwhile Rui Costa and Rivaldo played behind Inzaghi, who got his first hat-trick for the club. Maybe if we had lost 4–0 I would have discarded the idea altogether. Instead, we next beat Bayern Munich 2–1 with the same formation against an excellent team led by

THE DREAM

Michael Ballack and with the great keeper Oliver Kahn at his peak. Of course, there were two more for Inzaghi. One was a tap-in after a neat Rivaldo–Seedorf one-two split the defence in half. Then there was a wonderful header from a brilliant Serginho cross. This goal was a surprise because I'd actually sent Serginho on as a defensive measure to hold the score to 1–1.

It was becoming clear to me that Inzaghi was one of those players who was always a big player on big nights. He was one to treasure in the mould of the great Paolo Rossi. There were obviously other great forwards who were more versatile and could do other things on the pitch. When I rate Inzaghi I do so against the ones whose only job is to score and score and score. Inzaghi lived on the shoulder of the last defender. The Alex Ferguson joke that Inzaghi was born offside may have been true. He just had a nose for goal, and a hunger for scoring that could never be satisfied. He was quick and alert enough to poach, his brain seemed to move faster than anyone around him, and he was skilful at meeting crosses with his head. Another important quality he had, which is often overlooked, was his bravery. Great strikers put themselves in danger, in places where they can easily get hurt by bigger defenders. The stats revealed that, in his hat-trick against Deportivo, the three shots covered a total distance of less than 20 metres. That's another way of saying that he was always in the right place at the right time. And that he always hit the target.

THE THIRD TIME, 2002-3

I'm reminded of something Emiliano Mondonico, his old coach at Atalanta, said of his young star: 'He wasn't in love with goals, goals were in love with him.' A player with that much goal hunger never liked being left out. He always wanted to be in the thick of it. Whenever I did stick him on the bench, he could be angry with me for ages. We'd become strangers. Several days might pass before he decided to talk to me again. What an asset for any football side that could field the players to supply him. Altogether he got eight in the group stage.

Meanwhile I had hit on my first-choice back four of Šimić, Nesta, Maldini and Kaladze. So I started to believe that the new system, born as a quick fix for a single game, was necessity's child. One great bonus of the new system, which I hadn't anticipated, was that it gave more room to the two players behind Inzaghi to express themselves. The system fitted the talent I had available to me. It seemed a pity to waste it. The style of these wins also fell in with the president's philosophy of putting on a show.

When Bayern came to the San Siro we played well and efficiently. They had eighteen shots, we had four. Once more we put them away 2-1 with two high-quality finishes from Serginho and Inzaghi. While Bayern finished bottom of the group, we topped it without too many problems. Having won the first four games, I had room to use several squad players in the two remaining games. This was an interesting lesson, as we shipped four goals and lost them both. We could afford it on that occasion, but it was a reminder to me that winning those first group games is always important.

Back then there was no opportunity to forget it. The Champions League was structured at the time as two consecutive mini-leagues. Once you got out of one pool, you were immediately thrown straight into another. Our second-phase group pitted us against other teams that had finished in the top two spots of their leagues. As well as Lokomotiv Moscow and Borussia Dortmund, I found myself back facing an old opponent I came to know well from my playing days at Milan – Real Madrid.

The Spanish club was at the dawn of its period of signing *galácticos*: the current stars, marshalled by the coach Vicente del Bosque, were Zinedine Zidane, Luís Figo and Raúl playing behind Fernando Morientes, with Roberto Carlos firing free kicks from long distance. Even without Ronaldo on the pitch, that's quite a lot to handle. Having been Zidane's coach, I had special reason to fear him. But we managed it when they came to the San Siro in November, containing them in a tight game that we won 1–0. On the break Shevchenko – Inzaghi was out injured – ran on to a 50-metre through-ball from Rui Costa deep in our half, which Sheva slotted past the keeper from the edge of the box.

Next, away to Dortmund, I decided to revert to two strikers playing in front of a diamond and was rewarded when Inzaghi pounced onto a through-ball from Seedorf. My other main memory, apart from Tomáš Rosický's fierce shot

THE THIRD TIME, 2002–3

bouncing dramatically back off the crossbar, was the antics of their keeper Jens Lehmann. First, he went walkabout outside the box to try and dispossess Rivaldo. Among a crowd of outfield players, he fetched up nearer to the halfway line than the goal and was sauntering back when Seedorf's lofted shot drifted just over. Then he turned up in our box at the end and even attempted an overhead kick. It's always said that keepers' brains are wired differently from everyone else's, and Lehman has lived up to that beyond any doubt. I've been very lucky with my goalkeepers over the years. I never had to rein in those sort of antics from Dida, for example, who is certainly one of the best in the position ever to come out of Brazil, and ended up playing over 300 games for Milan.

Then came two 1–0 wins over Lokomotiv Moscow, which meant we were definitely through, allowing me to rest some key players for the game in Madrid. They needed the result more than us and we could afford to be put to the sword 3–1. We also lost to Dortmund. But still we finished top, giving us the slight advantage in the quarter-final. These things are always marginal, but the draw would pit us against a club that had finished runner-up in their group.

That team turned out to be Ajax. There was every reason to fear them, not least because up front they had a tall 21-year-old Swede called Zlatan Ibrahimović, although he turned out not to be an issue on the day. It was now April 2003. My problem was that Pirlo had had a knock in training which meant that he would miss both the quarter-final and, if we reached it, probably the semi-final too. Then Seedorf picked up an injury in Amsterdam. That first leg – a dull and cautious 0–0 stalemate – could not have been in greater contrast to the second leg. With those two crucial players missing, and Gattuso suspended (he had picked up a yellow card in the first leg which, on totting up, meant he would miss the second leg), I had to reconstruct my entire midfield and started off with a safety-first mindset. I drafted in two defensive replacements and hoped to stop Ajax getting that crucial away goal. In the first half Inzaghi lost his marker and stabbed in a good header from a Shevchenko cross. Then the game simply exploded. Jari Litmanen found himself in space to tap in a cross to give them the away-goal advantage. Two minutes later Inzaghi slipped down the left, and his deflected cross sat up nicely for Shevchenko to head in. Then Ajax equalised again in a goalmouth scramble.

The camera caught me smoking a cigarette earlier in the game. I'm not sure how many I got through that night, but this had now become a test for the nerves. (Later in my career I gave up nicotine and took to chewing gum in games instead.) In the last ten minutes I threw caution to the wind and sent on three attacking players to try and steal the tie. Salvation arrived in the very last seconds when Maldini sent a long ball up from the left-back position to Massimo Ambrosini, who nodded it into the box. Inzaghi latched on to the bobbling ball and cleverly lobbed it over the keeper. Tomasson, one of the players I'd sent on, made absolutely certain

THE THIRD TIME, 2002-3

it went over the line by following up and tapping in from all of six inches.

Obviously I was pleased with the outcome, but this was far from how I had seen the match playing out in my head. The plan was to control the game and keep a clean sheet. I would have been quite content with 1-0. Instead, Ajax, coached by Ronald Koeman, were great when they had possession and so I had to make do with an eleventh-hour 3-2. So much for plans. It's how a team handles itself when plans are disrupted that is the real challenge. I always remind my players that nothing is settled until the referee says so. So it proved. We got lucky and handled it. Just.

If the sterile first leg was the kind of game that critics blame on the away-goal rule, it was nothing compared to our semi-final. Fate had drawn us against our greatest rivals, Internazionale. These footballing enmities exist in every city where there's a choice of more than one big club to support. But there's something extra spicy when you share not just a city but a stadium, as we did at the San Siro. We found ourselves in the unusual situation of playing an away leg at home. Of course, we were used to occupying the visitors' dressing room once a season in Serie A. But because of the away-goal rule, this was different.

The atmosphere in the city was unlike anything I'd ever known. Our league encounters were always bad enough – the players found that they dominated every day of their lives for a month beforehand. At least we had only two weeks

THE DREAM

of anticipation this time, but this was a supercharged derby on another level. The only thing that could have made it more intense for the two clubs would be if it were to contest the final. The semi-final was bad enough.

At least we had Seedorf back. The medics predicted a two-month recovery period, but they didn't know Seedorf. He was a beast, and he was back. Pirlo's replacement Ambrosini was suspended so I put Cristian Brocchi at the base of the diamond. My big instruction was to the full-backs to hold back. The striker I was worried about was Hernán Crespo, the Argentine I'd coached at Parma who was as much of a goal machine as Inzaghi. Meanwhile at the other end they had Fabio Cannavaro, another of my old Parma players. To score we would have to get past him and his Azzurri teammate Marco Materazzi.

While my priority was to stop them scoring, the president's was to see us scoring, and he stormed into the dressing room at half-time and ordered me to make a tactical shift. 'You have to change the full-backs because they're not pushing.' He said this in front of the players, which I can't say I appreciated. But I knew how to handle him.

'OK, it's fine, you can go,' I replied. 'I'm going to change the full-backs.' Of course, I did no such thing, and the game finished without us conceding an away goal or scoring ourselves. I remember there was quite a lot of shooting from distance. Berlusconi wasn't happy but our relationship was good, and everything was forgotten the next day.

THE THIRD TIME, 2002–3

I won't say the second leg was any less tense or nervy, but as the away team we tried to be more positive, and it helped that we had Pirlo back. On the stroke of half-time Seedorf slid a clever ball through to Shevchenko, who wrong-footed the full-back and beat the keeper, and we were effectively in charge of the tie. As the home team, Inter would have to score twice to get past us. Everything went according to plan until ten minutes from the end. The Inter substitute Obafemi Martins went up for a high ball with Maldini and it somehow bounced off his shoulder, allowing him to run on and score. He then launched into a display of somersaulting that wouldn't disgrace an Olympic gymnast. I emptied the subs' bench to pack the defence and, despite a couple of close calls, we held on. Those last minutes were tough.

It's ties like this that reveal true character. Look at the team sheets of both sides and they're full of players who would go on to hold positions of responsibility beyond the world of coaching. I'm thinking of Javier Zanetti, who became a long-serving vice president at Inter, and Paolo Maldini, who was technical director at Milan. Rui Costa became president of Benfica. Shevchenko has been a powerful advocate for Ukrainian sport since the Russian invasion. Perhaps most impressively, in 2017 Kakha Kaladze became the mayor of Tbilisi in his native Georgia. They were all good footballers partly because they could shoulder responsibility, and partly because they were good thinkers who could keep their cool.

THE DREAM

Having survived the intense pressure of duelling with one local rival, we now discovered that the fates had another treat in store for us. Three of the four semi-finalists of that year's Champions League came from Italy, and the winners of the other semi-final match were Juventus. So to win the whole thing, we were going to have to beat a second rival. For everyone at the club this meant a great deal. For me, it had a personal significance. Two years earlier Juventus had let me go because I had failed to win the Champions League. Now my job was to make sure they failed again.

Finals between clubs from the same country are not really what European competition was created to bring about. But as the winners automatically qualified to defend their trophy, it was theoretically possible even before the Champions League replaced the European Cup. Somehow it never happened until 2000, when Real Madrid and Valencia both reached the final. It has since become a regular occurrence: Chelsea and Manchester United met in 2008, Bayern and Dortmund in 2013, Real and Atlético Madrid in 2014 and 2016, Liverpool and Tottenham Hotspur in 2019, Chelsea and Manchester City in 2021. But back in 2003 it still felt like an exceptional event.

The Juventus side had both changed and not changed since my time. Marcello Lippi, who I had replaced, had now replaced me. Edgar Davids was still a forceful presence in midfield, and Alessandro del Piero was the figurehead and captain. His regular partner up front was David Trezeguet, who I'd mainly used as a back-up. They'd since bought Gigi

THE THIRD TIME, 2002-3

Buffon and Lilian Thuram, both players I'd coached at Parma and both now in their prime.

The final was to take place at Old Trafford in Manchester. We went into the game with an unexpected advantage. I had no selection worries and was able to field my two first-choice strikers ahead of my first-choice midfield diamond. In defence Costacurta played out of position at right back and managed 65 minutes. He had intended to retire before the start of the season but fortunately he was persuaded to sign for one last season and at 36 he was still a valuable player for me. He continued to sign one-year extensions and even played in the Champions League at the age of 40; what a player!

The real star of Juventus, and the source of a lot of their creative threat, was the dynamic Czech midfielder Pavel Nedvěd. He was that season's winner of the Ballon d'Or and, luckily for us, he was suspended. This impacted on my tactics because Lippi decided to replace him on the left side of midfield with the right back Gianluca Zambrotta and move his centre back Paolo Montero to left back. With not one but two men playing out of position on their left, I decided to exploit that weakness by encouraging Shevchenko and Rui Costa to target that area of the pitch.

Honestly, it was not a great game. It was probably stifled for both sides by an overriding fear of defeat, and by the tactical changes that were necessary. Maybe I could have been more attacking. But it's not easy to break down a team comprised of five out-and-out defenders led by the formidable Ciro Ferrara, plus two defensive midfielders. Inzaghi had no luck against his old team-mates. His best effort was a header that, with incredibly fast reactions, Buffon tipped around the post. In the second half they hit the bar. With 20 minutes to go I took off Pirlo, whose passes could find no way through or over such a packed rearguard, and replaced him with Serginho in the hope that he would add energy.

Any gain this might have brought was negated by the fact that Roque Júnior, brought on for the injured Costacurta, himself got injured as well. So we were effectively playing with ten men. Fortunately, with extra time approaching, they were just as exhausted as us. My last change was to replace Rui Costa with Ambrosini. Almost nothing happened in extra time to threaten either goal and so I found myself facing yet another penalty shoot-out.

This one was different to the shoot-outs I had watched in Rome in 1984 and Pasadena in 1994. Both those finals were decided by penalties that kept flying over the bar. No one missed the target on this occasion, but the drama that played out was a reflection of the two hours that had gone before. There was a timidity in front of goal. It was as if no one wanted to score. And the goalkeepers were both dominant. In selecting the penalty takers, I had created a problem for the team when I had substituted the players who would have taken the penalties to protect us against conceding

THE THIRD TIME, 2002-3

in normal time. Two of the players who stepped up were defenders. Maybe this was a mistake.

I had wanted Shevchenko to go first but he insisted on going last. I always wanted the best to go first. Inzaghi always wanted to go at number six – don't ask me why. Serginho went first and happily he scored. Then Trezeguet and Seedorf, who you'd expect to score as well, didn't. Alessandro Birindelli equalised and then there was a sequence of no fewer than three saves. Perhaps nowadays the referee might take a closer look at the goalkeepers' movements. By the time Montero had completed his run-up and struck the ball, Dida was halfway to the edge of the six-yard box, thus greatly narrowing the angles. Nesta and Del Piero then scored, leaving it up to Shevchenko to settle it.

He was very emotional after the victory. 'Only one thing went through my mind. I put it exactly where I wanted to. I thought about everything when I was about to take the penalty. My childhood in Chernobyl, my friends who died, everything. I stared at the referee because the noise of the fans covered everything else, and I had not heard the whistle. He nodded to me, and I started. When the ball was halfway, I saw Buffon going the opposite direction. I understood before anyone else that it was done, that image will remain with me forever.' He later told anyone who would listen that it was the most important goal he had ever scored.

It was an important goal in my life too! Thanks to winning the shoot-out 3-2, we had given Milan its first

THE DREAM

Champions League since Capello won it nine years earlier. I am sometimes asked if I was happy to beat Juve after my less-than-happy time there. I cannot deny that it was good to take the trophy back to the San Siro, past the noses of my former employers.

It was a dream to become a professional footballer, and a dream to win the European Cup as a player on the pitch. To win my first Champions League in my first full season as coach at Milan was yet another dream come true. The achievement has a special flavour, enhanced by the fact that, after we'd beaten another Italian team in the semi-final, this was a final between two Italian teams. Italian football was at a peak. It was good for Serie A and good for Italy. And it was good for the president. I had done my job: I had made Berlusconi happy. Before the game I had 'allowed' the president into the dressing room. And now he came back wearing a very big smile.

9
FROM LA CORUÑA... TO ISTANBUL, 2003-5

That smile was still there when three days later we won the Coppa Italia. There was an extra cause for satisfaction. In the two legs played either side of the trip to Manchester, I rested a lot of players. Not one of my Champions League team started the first leg away against Roma, and we still won 4-1. Back at the San Siro, with half of the first team restored, we drew 2-2. It was a big squad effort.

And the following season it got better. We won the Scudetto at a canter. This was a personal vindication for me, because I was finally able to answer a criticism that had often been made of me. People said I was good in the drama of knockout competition but could not maintain momentum for the duration of a whole league season. Milan didn't lose their first game until just before Christmas and lost a second only on the penultimate weekend of the season. We finished 11 points ahead of Roma. Our tally of 82 points was a Serie A record. So for the first time in my coaching career, after

THE DREAM

nine seasons of trying, I had won a league championship at last.

But this is the story of my relationship with the Champions League. The goal, of course, was to win it again. The records show that this was a tall order. Several clubs had made it to consecutive finals, but none had managed to sit at the very top of Europe for two seasons running since Milan did it when I was a player. That was back in 1990. And the last side to have done it before then was Nottingham Forest in 1980. It was now 2003–4. Our draw was favourable for the group phase. We didn't set the continent alight but did enough. We beat Ajax 1–0 twice, won and lost 1–0 to Club Brugge, though earned only one point against Celta Vigo. By the time they beat us in the final round of games, we had already topped the group.

There was a change in the format of the competition that season. Instead of a second set of group games, there was now a round of 16. As a fan of the Champions League, I actually preferred the previous way of doing it, as it delivered on the promise of offering more matches between the biggest sides. But I did understand that it would be necessary to reduce the number of games played in domestic football, and this was a pill that no football association was ready to swallow then.

Our opponents were Sparta Prague. It was 0–0 away in the first leg, and there were no goals in the first half at the San Siro until injury time, when Inzaghi on the near

FROM LA CORUÑA ... TO ISTANBUL, 2003–5

post cleverly looped a header into the far corner. Sparta Prague equalised, putting them in the driving seat, but then Shevchenko got two. There's a clip of me leaping off my feet and punching the air, even straying quite a long way over the touchline. It looks like ecstasy but probably is more like relief. Gattuso thundered in a fourth with five minutes to go.

And then came the quarter-finals, and Deportivo. The auguries were good for this one. We had beaten them 4–0 away only the previous season. There was an extra reason to be confident, because we had an even stronger squad than the year before. Any team can benefit from improvements. We had lost two Brazilians in the shape of Rivaldo and Roque Júnior but gained two in Cafu and Kaká. Both were upgrades who brought great strengths, but they were very different sorts of acquisitions. Cafu was immensely experienced. Now 33, he had captained Brazil to their recent World Cup win and won the Scudetto with Roma. Their fans nicknamed him Il Pendolino because he was like an express train running up and down the right flank. I admit that when he joined us the average age of our defence went up, given that Costacurta and Maldini were also well into their mid-thirties. But he still had bags of energy. And without making any sacrifices defensively, he gave us an extra width and pace that we had slightly lacked on the right side of the pitch.

As for Kaká, he was only 21 when he arrived but he was already good enough to be a first-choice pick. When I first saw Kaká as he arrived in Milan, he looked like a university student with his neat dress sense and glasses. But when I saw him play, I was lost for words. I didn't know how to describe what I was seeing. In his first training session, he faced off against Gattuso and then Nesta and neither could stop him. We had taken his student glasses off, put him in a football kit, and he had become a phenomenon. It was like Superman emerging from the telephone kiosk. He played 45 games that season, as many as Seedorf and Gattuso in midfield. No one in the squad played more. His arrival did, I admit, recreate the same headache I'd had the previous season trying to accommodate Rivaldo. The difference was that Kaká was approaching greatness, rather than Rivaldo who was no longer at his peak. There was something in the way that Kaká moved around the space in front of the penalty area that put me in mind of Michel Platini. At times he was unmarkable. But still, how do you fit Pirlo, Seedorf, Rui Costa and Kaká into the same team? The answer is you don't. I told all of them that they had to help me solve the riddle or they would spend some time on the bench. That season Kaká came off the bench five times, Rui Costa fourteen. I more or less fitted them all in by creating a diamond with Pirlo at the base and Kaká further forward.

With Serginho and Dida already part of the squad, AC Milan now had a strong Brazilian flavour to match the Dutch style that characterised the team when I played for it. Rivaldo had cancelled his contract and returned to play in Brazil. But he soon returned to Europe and was to have an interesting coda to his career in Greece, where he scored a lot of goals for Olympiacos and then AEK Athens. One of them in particular could have had a big impact on his old team-mates, but I'll get to that in a bit.

The team was maturing. The players' performances were more cerebral, more nuanced and had more variety. They were able to control games more effectively. Possession became as important a defensive weapon as it was in attack. The aim was to be efficient, to get the maximum reward for the minimum effort. And mostly it worked.

But it failed spectacularly in the Champions League. In the first leg against Deportivo at the San Siro, the result shows that we played like the favourites to hold on to our title. In actual fact we let them score first with a near-post header. To say we would come to regret that away goal is an understatement. For the whole first half we were a bit toothless in front of goal until in two smooth movements Kaká controlled a Cafu cross and volleyed it in. Suddenly we were awake. That was just before half-time. Just after it, Shevchenko doubled our tally. Three minutes later Kaká drilled a shot in from the edge of the box to make it three. In another four minutes Pirlo added a fourth with a spectacular free kick. Four goals in eight minutes. It just shows that anything can happen on a football pitch in a very short space of time. As I would discover to my cost soon enough.

Obviously, the tie was not over, but this was a strong lead to take with us to Spain. Turning over a three-goal lead is not impossible, but it is rare. And remember, we had won

THE DREAM

here 4–0 the previous season. You wouldn't say that they fielded a team full of superstars. Mauro Silva at the defensive base of the midfield was 36. Juan Carlos Valerón was a Spain international. All the same, the mood in the Deportivo stadium went up a notch when their Uruguayan striker Pandiani, who'd got their goal in the first leg, did it again with a neat turn after five minutes. Then they just kept on scoring. There were two more before half-time.

The second half was dominated by one big question: could they seal the tie? I wanted to re-establish some sense of stability so just after Pirlo got booked, I replaced him with Serginho. Then in search of an away goal I sent on Inzaghi for Tomasson. Inzaghi was on the bench as he had needed a rest and Tomasson had needed the minutes, so the selection had made sense with the lead we took into the second leg. It didn't make sense now. But nothing seemed to change. Deportivo's midfielder Fran rifled a shot that caught Cafu's outstretched boot and was deflected in when Dida dived in the opposite direction. The stadium went crazy. With about 20 minutes to go I had one last card to play. I sent on Rui Costa for left back Giuseppe Pancaro, and it nearly worked. He smashed a powerful long shot that called for an athletic save. As the final whistle blew we all looked at each other as if in a trance. What had just happened?

After our elimination, the media and everyone else asked that same question. What the hell happened? The answer was – and it still is – that I don't know. It's difficult

FROM LA CORUÑA . . . TO ISTANBUL, 2003–5

to explain. Did I disrespect the opposition by making some team changes? Did the team suffer psychologically thanks to that early and well-taken goal? These things can change the mentality and once that happens it can be difficult to get back. Somehow the dynamic of the game goes over to them and, whatever you try, it becomes hard to change the flow. What can I say? When it is so strange and unexpected it is difficult to know what lessons to draw. We were up against a very good team who played very well, and some very experienced and very good players made mistakes. It happens. It's the beauty of football. You just never know.

As a lesson in the cruelty of football, our night in La Coruña was just an appetiser. The domestic season ended in glory with my first Scudetto as coach. Then several of my players went off to Portugal for the Euros. The Italians – Pirlo, Gattuso and Nesta – came back sooner than they would have liked. They were eliminated by an inferior goal difference after finishing level in their group with Denmark and Sweden. Ibrahimović got an equaliser against them with five minutes left. So at least they had a longer amount of holiday time in which to rest up. Portugal got all the way to the final and, surprisingly, came up against Greece. Rui Costa came on for the last 30 minutes, just after Greece got what turned out to be the winner.

Greek football had a more immediate effect upon my year a few months later. Olympiacos were drawn in the same Champions League group as Liverpool, who had to come through a qualifying round. In the sixth and final match of the group Liverpool were home at Anfield to face the Greeks, having lost to them away, and needed to win by two clear goals. By that time Rivaldo was back in Europe and doing well at Olympiacos. He scored from a free kick in the first half and suddenly Liverpool had to score three. Sound familiar? But Steven Gerrard had one of those 'Stevie G' games, topped off by a third goal that was driven on the half volley from outside the box. 'I honestly don't know how we did that,' he said afterwards. Every Milan fan would soon come to wish they hadn't. Deportivo, our other nemesis, finished bottom of that group on two points. They didn't score a single goal. Oh well.

As for our group, it took us a long time to break down Shaktar Donetsk, which took Shevchenko back for a rare game in Ukraine. Eventually Seedorf got our winner. Then we beat Celtic 3–1 at home thanks to two very late goals from Inzaghi and Pirlo. Also we had back-to-back games against Barcelona which would probably determine who finished top of the group. However spicy it looked to the fans and neutrals, to me there was a sentimental subplot because Barca was coached by my old partner in central midfield, Frank Rijkaard. We had many happy memories of competing together and shared those memories when we met before and after the games. We are still good friends. But then we were in opposition, and in suits. Everything had changed.

Our teams were well matched, but a lone Shevchenko header won it for us at home. At the Nou Camp he did it again, running on to a superb lofted ball from Pirlo. But they

FROM LA CORUÑA . . . TO ISTANBUL, 2003–5

had some very good players. First Xavi rolled a very canny pass into the path of Samuel Eto'o, who buried it with one touch. It looked as if we were going to leave town with a draw until Ronaldinho received the ball just outside the D, dinked it to his left, wrong-footed a couple of our defenders and smashed it into the top left corner. You can't keep a player like that quiet for just 89 minutes. It has to be the whole 90.

But we got a win and a draw in our last two games and topped the group by three points. One of the exciting things about the 4–0 home win over Shaktar was the two goals scored by Crespo, who had had an unhappy time at Chelsea and arrived on a season-long loan. I knew him from when he was a younger player at Parma and I thought I could get the best out of him. It was useful to have an extra striker with great poaching instincts to call on because that year Inzaghi twice had to have ankle surgery – it was why he was missing from the Azzurri squad at the Euros.

Meanwhile at the back we had Jaap Stam, who we'd bought from Lazio. I kept my interest in him a secret from the media but then my son, Davide, who was then 15, heard me denying that I had my eye on him and actually blew my cover.

'But Papi, why don't you buy him?' he asked in front of some journalists. 'You're always talking about him.'

Stam wasn't always first choice – Nesta and Maldini played quite a few more games than him that season – but his power and experience were very useful assets to call on as Costacurta was not getting any younger (if we got to the final of

THE DREAM

the Champions League, he would be 39). Although he was already in his thirties, Stam still brought down the average age of the defence when he played. If I fielded a back four of Maldini, Costacurta, Nesta and Cafu – I can't remember if I ever did – their combined age would come to 136.

In the round of 16 we were up against Stam's old club Manchester United. We went there first, and in the eyes of many it was a case of United's young strikers versus Milan's old legs. Actually, I'd come up against a lot of the United players six years earlier, in 1999, when Juventus played against them in the semi-final. The likes of Scholes, Keane and Giggs were now in their thirties. The sharpness was in the legs of Cristiano Ronaldo and Wayne Rooney and, when he started in the second leg, Ruud van Nistelrooy. Our old men at the back managed to stop them scoring for 180 minutes. Maldini, centre back in the first leg and left back in the second, was immense as both an inspiring leader and a calm organiser. Yet again he proved that he really is one of the greatest defenders of all time.

The first leg was a game with more energy expended than chances created. United didn't seriously threaten our goal, and in the first half Seedorf clipped the bar with a thunderous free kick. Deep into the second his fierce shot was badly spilled by their keeper and Crespo pounced. Back at the San Siro Crespo was the difference again, meeting a Cafu cross with a brilliant long-range header that ballooned over their keeper (a different one).

FROM LA CORUÑA ... TO ISTANBUL, 2003-5

If that was a gruelling war of attrition, our quarter-final proved to be much easier than we could have anticipated. It was Milan against Inter again, with all the drama that this entailed. Our semi-final two seasons earlier had been incredibly tight, and it seemed wise to expect more of the same, even though Cannavaro was no longer the rock at the heart of their defence, having left for Juventus. In fact, it was dramatic for an unexpected reason. We beat them 2-0 in the home leg with goals from Stam and Shevchenko, both heading in free kicks from Pirlo. By half-time in the second leg we had added another goal from Shevchenko, whose curling left-footed drive flew in from a distance.

But with less than 20 minutes to go, and Milan leading 3-0 on aggregate, homemade flares were hurled onto the pitch from behind our goal by the home fans. The referee stopped play twice and appeals were made to the Inter fans to desist. Then a flare struck Dida on the shoulder. Our penalty area looked like a war zone. The game was abandoned, and we were awarded an extra two goals by UEFA. It was a strange reversal of fortune for Maldini, Costacurta and me. The 3-0 scoreline was a flashback to when Galliani refused to let us come out and finish the game at Marseille back in 1991. Inter were fined and ordered to play their next four European games behind closed doors.

The semi-final seemed less daunting. PSV Eindhoven did not look a threat on paper and at home we managed to brush them aside 2-0 with yet another goal from Shevchenko and a second from Tomasson, both profiting from the passing of Kaká. In the second leg I left Shevchenko to forage alone up front and packed the midfield. But things did not go our way and with 90 minutes played the tie was level. Then with extra time bearing down, Kaká ghosted down the left and sent an inch-perfect cross for Ambrosini to glance in. PSV immediately got one back but we had our precious away goal and were through by a whisker.

And so to Istanbul. The date – 25 May 2005 – is burned into the memories of all fans who were there as well as the millions watching on TV.

What went wrong in the final against Liverpool is one of the great mysteries that makes football what it is. If there was a worry, it was that our league campaign had tailed off in April after we had stayed close to Juventus all the way through the season. Fatigue was setting in, so I rested regulars for the final game of Serie A. And yet there were reasons to be confident. Liverpool were back in the final for the first time since they beat Roma on penalties, with me watching from the stand, 21 years earlier, in 1984. Against Manchester United we had overcome a seemingly stronger English side that contained more proven match-winners. The likes of Harry Kewell and Milan Baroš were good players, but they were not Ronaldo and Rooney, who we had successfully fended off. Their goalkeeper Jerzy Dudek was known to make mistakes too. Steve Finnan, Jamie Carragher, Sami Hyppiä and John Arne Riise made a solid back four, but they

FROM LA CORUÑA ... TO ISTANBUL, 2003–5

were not Cafu, Nesta, Stam and Maldini. The heart of the team was in midfield where Xabi Alonso played alongside Gerrard. It was Gerrard we knew we were going to have to worry about but we were confident that Gattuso and Seedorf could cope with him.

As for Milan, I selected a very strong eleven full of winners. Maldini was playing in his seventh final. Seedorf had won it with three different clubs. Moving Maldini to left back, I had Stam and Nesta in central defence with Cafu at right back. In midfield Pirlo played at the base of a diamond behind Seedorf and Gattuso, with Kaká serving Shevchenko and Crespo. I left Inzaghi, who had been injured for so much of the season, out of the match-day squad.

Our superiority and greater experience played out as the pundits all predicted. Even Gerrard agreed. 'They've got the best players in the world,' he would say later. 'We weren't as good as them.' I genuinely think of those first 45 minutes as the best display of footballing excellence that any side I have coached has ever produced in a final – or in any other game for that matter. Pressing them into submission, we seemed to be able to win back possession at will. We were unstoppable. By half-time we were 3–0 up.

We were on song from the very first minute when Maldini scored with a great right-foot strike to convert a difficult cross from a Pirlo free kick. It was perfectly crafted with decoy runners and blockers opening up the space, almost on the penalty spot, into which Maldini arrived unmarked.

THE DREAM

At 36, he became the oldest ever scorer in a Champions League final. Sometimes early is too soon but the ball kept flowing forward towards Liverpool's goal. Pirlo was vertically feeding Kaká between the lines, from the bottom of the diamond straight through to the top. Kaká then either ran with the ball or fed the front players. It was devastating.

And the goals just got better and better. The second came when we turned over Liverpool possession for the umpteenth time and immediately countered with Kaká carrying the ball straight at the retreating Liverpool defence before transferring it to Shevchenko, who had broken into an inside right position. Uncharacteristically and surprisingly for a goal scorer, Sheva rolled the ball across to Crespo, who calmly tapped it into the back of the Liverpool net.

The third goal was even more beautiful. Kaká cut their defence in half with a pass so accurately weighted into Crespo's path that without breaking stride he was able to clip it with the outside of his right foot beyond the onrushing Dudek.

But every match, as I never stop saying, is contested over 90 minutes. Or failing that, 120 minutes. Failing that, over a penalty shoot-out. It is never over until it is over. In the half-time break I told them just that. The game was not over yet, but it would be if we scored a couple more goals. Just to set the record straight, we were not celebrating in the dressing room at half-time. In fact, the reverse is true. I was telling the players to start again as if from the beginning, to continue

FROM LA CORUÑA . . . TO ISTANBUL, 2003–5

and not to think about the first half, to finish the final, to kill the game.

Their coach, Rafa Benítez, must have said something incredibly inspirational, because they came out with fire in their bellies. Their supporters welcomed them back onto the pitch with a stirring rendition of 'You'll Never Walk Alone'. For them it wasn't all over, and they had nothing to lose.

At half-time, Benítez replaced Finnan at right back with Didi Hamann in defensive midfield, altering Liverpool's set-up to 3–5–2. This wasn't a case of tactical genius as has been suggested. It was simply an effort to match our midfield numbers and stop the waves of our attacks. Although it was essentially a defensive move, the arrival of Hamman did release Gerrard into a more attacking position and enabled the wide players, Riise and Vladimir Šmicer, to engage our full-backs. And then it started to happen.

Everybody loved Gerrard and wanted to sign him, including me, but he loved Liverpool too much. The reshuffled formation allowed him to change the game by himself. It was one of those displays that only great players are capable of. Our great players had given us a three-goal lead and we were still in control for the majority of the game – with the exception, of course, of the period between the 54th and 60th minutes. Maybe the first goal should have been a red flag. Šmicer lifted a cross into the box from the left and Gerrard was on the end of it, unmarked in our penalty area. His powerful header from the penalty spot flew beyond Dida

THE DREAM

and he was already running back for the restart, geeing up his team-mates as he ran. This was true captaincy. In retrospect Gattuso suggested that the whole side froze with fear. That was on 54 minutes. But we were playing so well that I imagined we would score more goals. There was no reason to panic, we were still two goals in front and still dominating. No substitution necessary. In hindsight I could have made a change at that point to affect the mentality of the game, to dampen the Liverpool enthusiasm, to kill the hope.

But within another two minutes Šmicer, also unchallenged, had a go from outside the box and somehow his shot pierced a crowded area and went in. It suddenly became clear what was happening. I had to make a defensive substitution, both to break up the game and to improve our defensive intensity. While I was doing that, and before I could get a sub on, Gerrard made a strong run into our box. His heel was clipped by Gattuso. Penalty. When Alonso stepped up to take it, Dida dived to his right and stopped the shot, but couldn't prevent the follow-up.

The 90 minutes ended 3–3. It was Deportivo all over again. Only this was the final. In six minutes Liverpool had levelled through sheer force of will. We had stunned them in the first minute. Now they had stunned us back.

It just goes to show that you can do everything right in terms of preparation, selection and tactics. But sometimes there are random variables over which no coach can have any influence. The random variable in this case was the

FROM LA CORUÑA ... TO ISTANBUL, 2003–5

passion of Gerrard, his team-mates and their fans. Then, at the very end of extra time, there was Dudek. Liverpool's defenders threw themselves in the way of everything, but it was their goalkeeper who saved the match for them, making a pair of incredible fast-reaction saves to deny Shevchenko with only three minutes left.

What was good about us that day was that we picked up our game again and should have still won the game. We dominated them for 114 minutes. We let them dominate us for six minutes. The mistakes that beat us were in those six minutes of madness in which we threw away our position. If I had acted differently maybe I could have sent a stronger message to my players after their first goal and changed things in a way that would have allowed them to regain their confidence and momentum. I always like to take a little time to think. It turned out that six minutes just wasn't enough thinking time; things happened too quickly. The result was penalties.

I had the same talk with Shevchenko. 'You take the first one.' 'No, let me have the last one.' The great strikers always want the last one, the glory one. I said, 'OK.' After all, he is Sheva, who am I to argue? So I selected Serginho to go first and Shevchenko last, as they had two years earlier in the final against Juventus. But I had more ball players on the pitch this time so didn't have to ask any defenders to step up. There were a couple of reminders of the 1985 shoot-out. One of our shots flying over the bar. Dudek wobbling his knees like a Bruce Grobbelaar tribute act (it didn't bother Kaká,

THE DREAM

who scored). Perhaps we were psychologically traumatised at a time when we needed to hold our nerve. Maybe it didn't help that Dudek was charging off the line before the penalties were taken. After two penalties each it was 2–0 to them. Then 2–1 after three. Then 3–2 after four. Shevchenko had to score to keep us in it. He sent it down the middle. Dudek, diving to his right, caught the shot with his trailing legs.

Ultimately, I have to accept that we played a marvellous final. We lost without deserving to lose and we had to accept our defeat. We were unhappy but I think we lost in an honourable way. After the game, everybody in the Milan camp seemed dazed. From the outside even the great Maradona seemed shocked. 'Even the Brazil team that won the 1970 World Cup could not have staged a comeback with Milan leading 3–0,' he said. 'I have seen comebacks like that in football but never against a team that was so clearly superior as Milan were.'

It became one of the most famous finals in the history of the competition, and unfortunately, I was the coach of the losing side. Was I angry? How could I be? Milan played wonderfully. On another night Dudek would have not stopped one or the other of those two late shots from Shevchenko, who did nothing wrong. I don't think I would have changed anything about the way we played. Sometimes you just don't win. But the thing is to keep trying. Sometimes the dream is just out of reach, you wake up before arriving at the final destination.

10

THE FOURTH TIME, 2005-7

If it's true, as they say, that you can learn more in defeat than in victory, then the Champions League was becoming a great teacher for me.

In the following two seasons the competition would have a different kind of drama in store for us. We had come so close in Istanbul that I didn't feel the need to make many changes to my squad. For my fourth full season at Milan – my fifth in total – I had to shuffle the deck a bit in defence because Maldini was injured for some of the season. Cafu wasn't always available either and Stam ended up playing some games at right back. In midfield Rui Costa, who turned 34 that season, was no longer a first-choice pick.

The main alterations to the squad were up front, where I recruited two powerful forwards. Christian Vieri, who had been such a major figure at Inter, jumped ship and joined us at Milan. Maybe there was a romantic idea that he could resume the strike partnership with Crespo both had enjoyed at his old club. But the years were catching up

THE DREAM

with him, and he had a legacy of injuries, so it was not a happy stay, and he didn't get many games. Alberto Gilardino was a stronger signing from Parma. It meant that we had to allow the departure of Jon Dahl Tomasson, who had impressed me with his exemplary work ethic in training despite the limited opportunities that came his way. He was a good soldier and would go on to win over a hundred caps for Denmark. I was proud to see him appointed manager of the Swedish national side in 2024.

The good news for me was that Shevchenko had not been psychologically affected by Istanbul. I promoted him to captain whenever Maldini or Costacurta were not playing, and he started scoring a lot of goals in a group that also included PSV, Schalke 04 and Fenerbahçe. Inzaghi was also back among the goals in the knockout rounds. He scored with two headers at the San Siro in the round of 16 against Bayern Munich, who we beat 5–2 on aggregate. And in the quarter-final he got two more at home against Olympique Lyonnais. That was a nailbiter, because with two minutes to go the score was 1–1, and they were on the brink of going through on their away goal. Then in the 88th minute something very unusual happened that suggested luck was on our side. Shevchenko's shot across goal struck the far post, then bounced back and hit the other post. Before anyone else could get to it Inzaghi stabbed it in from a yard out. Shevchenko made sure of the result in the 90th minute, breaking into the box and rounding the keeper to score.

THE FOURTH TIME, 2005–7

So for the second year running we were back in the semi-final, and up against Barcelona and my old team-mate Frank Rijkaard – again we spent an enjoyable time together recalling old friends and old times. The result was two superb games of intense, high-quality attrition football. We were very well matched, and over the three hours of combat there was absolutely nothing to divide us bar a single act of genius. We had our own maestro in Pirlo, who was now developing into a truly world-class player at the base of our midfield diamond. At the San Siro we certainly started as the better side, but we paid for our lack of precision in front of goal.

After nearly an hour on the clock, Ronaldinho produced that moment of genius. He had not been able to shake off the attentions of Gattuso, who had been detailed to man-to-man mark him, but halfway between the centre circle and the D he tried a stepover. But that didn't fool Gattuso, so he turned his back then turned again, looked up and sent a delicate chip into space in the left-hand side of the box. It was almost like a soft golf shot onto the green. It bounced up perfectly for Ludovic Giuly to turn and lash it in before Dida could move a muscle.

There was always the second leg. They had won at the San Siro, so why couldn't we win at Nou Camp? We wouldn't need a miracle, but we would need an extraordinary performance to get through. The game had everything but the goal. It was end-to-end entertainment in which attacks and defences tested each other to the limit. Dida bravely kept us in the game with several great saves. So did the Barca player Juliano Belletti when he somehow failed to connect with an absolute sitter. Shevchenko very nearly took the game into extra time with a great header that was harshly disallowed for an alleged foul on Carles Puyol. This angered me at the time, and looking back at the replay I still can't see what he did wrong as there was barely any contact before Puyol tumbled to the floor. But in truth, even if VAR had been available, the decision would probably not have been overturned. We were close, but not close enough. I was happy at least for Rijkaard that Barcelona went on to beat Arsenal in the final in Paris.

Meanwhile, that season was dominated by a scandal that enveloped Italian football. It became known as *Calciopoli*, and it involved the discovery of improper contact between referee associations and certain football executives. It was proved that some clubs had attempted to arrange for favourable referees to be put in charge of some games. The story broke at the end of 2005–6, but also covered the previous season. Juventus was stripped of its Scudetti for both seasons and automatically relegated. This was an extraordinary thing to happen to a club whose size and influence could be measured in what happened at that summer's World Cup. No fewer than eight Juventus players featured in the final that took place in Berlin: four for Italy, four for France. Italy had better luck in the shoot-out than when I was assistant coach in the 1994 final. Pirlo scored with the first penalty, and every other Azzurro did too.

THE FOURTH TIME, 2005–7

Unfortunately, Milan was implicated in *Calciopoli*. The original punishment was to have 30 points deducted at the start of the 2006–7 season. With such a handicap I knew it would be impossible to qualify for the Champions League as there was no way we could finish high enough. However, UEFA also banned us from the current season's competition, so I allowed the players to go on their holidays. That ban was then overturned when it was ruled that UEFA did not have the legal right to compound the Italian FA's ban with their own. They were not pleased and issued a terse statement: 'UEFA wish to make it clear to the club that this admission [to the competition] is far from being given with the utmost conviction.'

So from the start of that season's Champions League the club was not popular with the game's administrators. It was very popular with me, however, as it meant there wouldn't be an exodus of players like there was at Juventus where many of the club's players were picked off by their rivals. But, more urgently, I had to recall the players from their holidays because the consequence of our downgraded punishment was that we were able to enter the Champions League, albeit in the final qualifying round. This was not necessarily a disaster for us. The last time we had done so, four years earlier against Slovan Liberec in August 2002, we went on to win the whole competition. The only problem was that the first game was scheduled to take place on 9 August. It was exactly one month after the World Cup final, which Pirlo had participated in. Three more Milan players were on the bench.

This was the worst possible preparation for such an important game. Cafu arrived back the day before the first leg at home to Red Star Belgrade. He hadn't even trained but still played the whole 90 minutes, running up and down the right flank like the beast he was. We won 1–0, then 2–1 away. Red Star were nothing like as strong as the side I played against in 1988, or which won the European Cup in 1991. Still, it was an unusual and uncomfortable way to start the campaign. The good news was that Inzaghi was back among the goals, scoring in both legs.

Our points deduction was reduced to 15 and then to 8. But the prospect of winning the Scudetto that season still seemed very remote, and even getting into the fourth qualifying place would be very difficult. So, although no one ever said this out loud, our main focus for the season was the Champions League.

Sadly, if we were going to win it, we would have to do so without the help of Shevchenko, who had decided to leave for Chelsea. Stam and Rui Costa also moved on. The question of how I was going to replace his goals, and his pace, was one I kept asking myself all season. Inzaghi was now 33. One solution that was hit upon in mid-season was to bring in the original Ronaldo on loan. When the Brazilian superstar arrived in the winter transfer window he completed a unique journey for a top footballer, having moved to Barcelona to

THE FOURTH TIME, 2005–7

Inter to Real to Milan. He had lost some of his explosive speed and power but still he scored a goal every other game in Serie A. Another Brazilian signing was Ricardo Oliveira, but it proved impossible for him to give his best after his sister was kidnapped in October 2006. Fortunately, she was released unharmed the following March.

The departure of Shevchenko proved to be the catalyst that enabled the final version of the Christmas Tree formation to be fully embraced. For most of the important games I sent out a formation with Inzaghi up front and, just behind him, Kaká and Seedorf, who now played in a more advanced position than he'd been used to. The success of the system was only possible because in each layer across the pitch there were players who could pass well through the lines. Pirlo could manage the possession, and in front of him Kaká moved really well in space. We had two good full-backs who could venture forward because Nesta and Maldini could be left to manage things at the back. Gattuso and Ambrosini were really strong defensively, so without the ball our full-backs enabled us to shift quickly from a diamond 4–4–2 to an attacking formation of 2–5–2–1. With that central five we would always outnumber the opposition with or without the ball.

I was aware that the formation had two potential drawbacks. First, there could be a lack of width. Second, we could be exposed in defence if the midfielders either side of Pirlo were pulled too wide to cover the flanks. But the flaws could also be strengths. The lack of perceived width was compensated for by the speed and work rate of the full-backs I had available to me. We were strengthened by the performances of our Czech left back Marek Jankulovski, who had arrived the previous season but now cemented his place in the side. And at right back there was Cafu or Massimo Oddo, who I signed from Lazio in the transfer window and was possibly a more accurate crosser. All were formidable in attack. Their ability to join up in that middle five enabled the three central midfielders to stay compact. The other great thing about the work rate of Ambrosini and Gattuso was that it freed Seedorf and Kaká to perform their magic further up the pitch where they could hurt the opposition.

Over and above these tactical considerations, there was something else that helped us. At a difficult moment for the club, I knew I could rely on the Milan family. Five years after I arrived to take up my position as coach at my old club alongside my team-mate Tassotti, a strong nucleus of the same group of players was still with me. There was a dozen of them in all: Maldini, Costacurta, Dida, Nesta, Kaladze, Serginho, Pirlo, Gattuso, Seedorf, Inzaghi, Šimić and Brocchi. That is unusual even among the top clubs. The sense of togetherness we felt was founded on all that time we had spent in one another's company. I'm not saying everything was perfect. No squad can hope for total harmony. I won't mention their names, but that season one fringe player tested positive for a banned substance, and a promising new signing struggled on the pitch because he failed to integrate

THE FOURTH TIME, 2005–7

with his new team-mates, but these are not unusual distractions. All things told there was a very strong camaraderie.

We needed that sense of togetherness because in Serie A things were not going well. We won our first three games, drew the next three and then lost three successive home games in the league for the first time in 40 years. Palermo beat us at the San Siro for the first time in their history. The defeat coincided with my decision to end the tradition of the pre-match *ritiro*. Instead of us all spending the night before the game at a hotel, we let the players go home. To be honest the *ritiro* was becoming outdated and I think I just hurried it along a little. Then we lost to Inter 4–3. It was a typical derby. Materazzi scored the winner and then was immediately sent off. Eight other players were booked.

Throughout all this, we were finding it very hard to score. There were rumours among fans and the media that I might be replaced. I can say with my hand on my heart that it didn't bother me. In football, when things don't go well, you sometimes pay the price. I knew it could happen, but I never felt under threat.

Probably the worst result was the last game in the Champions League group phase. The draw was kind, pitting us against the relatively unthreatening trio of Lille, AEK Athens and Anderlecht. We had little trouble sticking to the plan of getting points in the bag early on, before I started to rotate the squad, which was partly forced on me by a lot of injuries all happening at once. We beat AEK 3–0, drew 0–0 with

THE DREAM

Lille, beat Anderlecht 1–0 away despite a second-half sending off, then 4–1 at home, helped by a Kaká hat-trick. This was enough to top the group even though we lost the last two games. The defeat to Lille was particularly bad. It was an ugly evening. We showed little determination, we were slow and we played as individuals. If you measure a team's determination to win by how many fouls it commits, it looked as if we couldn't care less. We committed only nine.

By December things were going badly enough that other teams started to hope they got us in the draw for the round of 16. Celtic drew the lucky ticket and were scheduled to welcome us to Glasgow on 20 February. This for me is the moment in the season when the Champions League really comes alive. And fortunately, by then we were no longer such a pushover. We had won the last six league games out of seven, scoring 16 goals. We had managed to remedy our problems.

One of the things that changed the course of our season was a break that took us to Malta. This was in the first half of January, when the Italian season briefly halts. We worked very well there, the team was in good spirits and we agreed that we wanted to forget all the negative things that had happened since August: the docked points, the bad performances. And I crossed my fingers that a lot of injured players would make it back onto the pitch.

But our scoring radar malfunctioned against Celtic. No goals after both legs, three hours of stalemate. We had made the greater effort to break the deadlock and had four times

THE FOURTH TIME, 2005–7

as many attempts on goal. I cannot disrespect their manager, Gordon Strachan, for choosing to play with a low block. After all, I am a disciple of Sacchi, and I have had success with that same strategy many times. To break them down we had to take the risk of keeping the full-backs high, which can make you vulnerable to counter-attacks. As the second leg at the San Siro got ever closer to extra time, we were attacking with all ten outfield players. But we couldn't find a way through. Maldini's point-blank header was blocked, a Seedorf shot was athletically saved and Kaká's drive bounced back off the bar. I was beginning to fear that we might end up having to decide it all on penalties.

I shouldn't have worried. Three minutes into extra time, Kaká broke the deadlock. They had defended so stoutly for so long but suddenly he had the pace to sprint clear of all defenders in the inside left channel and slot his shot through their keeper's legs. It was a tough tie, and Kaká was the difference. And so, we were in the quarter-finals. If we weren't having our very best season, we were at least doing better than all of the previous season's quarter-finalists. None of the others had made it back to the same round this year.

Not that this meant there were any easy ties. Next up were Bayern Munich, who came to the San Siro in early April. The encouraging news was that I had most of my first-choice players back, including Nesta, who hadn't played for a while. Pirlo put us ahead in the first half with a very unusual goal for him. A deep ball into the box wrong-footed their defence and he looped a header over Oliver Kahn. Kaká won a penalty and scored with six minutes to go. But either side of it we conceded two scrappy away goals, including one deep into injury time.

This at least made it clear what we'd have to do in Munich: we had to win. In the end we found the task surprisingly easy. They started well but we were calm and disciplined and got two away goals, Seedorf and Inzaghi both scoring from more or less the same spot on the edge of the box. Bayern put us under a lot of pressure, but we managed to keep them quiet. In statistical terms we were a model of efficiency. They enjoyed nearly 60 per cent of the possession and had more than twice as many shots. The more important statistic for me was that Inzaghi had scored for the first time in two and a half months.

As we advanced into a semi-final for the fourth time in five years, the only conclusion you could draw was that the intense heat of European competition was our natural habitat. We liked the Champions League, and the Champions League seemed to like us. And, to be honest, I needed the success in it because by that stage of the season Inter had already won the Scudetto and our president was impatient for another trophy. He even gathered the club's players and staff together and demanded we end the season on a high. 'I want a month of the old Milan,' he said.

The semi-final brought us face to face with Alex Ferguson's Manchester United. The last time I'd taken them on

THE FOURTH TIME, 2005–7

at this stage was back in 1999 with Juventus. In recent years their dominance of English football was not quite as strong as it had been. They hadn't won the Premiership for four years, although they were about to win it three times in a row. Their stars were Rooney and Cristiano Ronaldo, fed by Giggs and Scholes, and it was this combination which managed to sneak a 3–2 win in a crazy game at Old Trafford.

Our plan was to counter-attack via our front three and rely on a resolute defensive screen. It didn't quite work out that way. The lead seemed to change hands every few minutes. First Ronaldo opened the scoring for United after just five minutes and then Kaká responded with two clever and well-taken goals to put us in front before half-time. His first was a combination of genius and comic effect in equal measures. First Kaká played the ball over Gabriel Heinze's head, then cushion-headed it past the oncoming Patrice Evra, who then ran into Heinze while Kaká was calmly sliding the ball past Edwin van der Sar in goal. Kaká looked behind him to see Patrice and Heinze climbing up off the pitch.

But they had Rooney, who was a special talent, as their lone striker. He scored once on the hour and then again in the first minute of injury time to give United a one-goal lead to take to Milan. At least we had two away goals. We were still alive.

For the return game my main tactical switch was to shift the position of Pirlo so that it was harder for Scholes to man-mark him all night. Our only changes were to bring in Kaladze for Maldini, who was unavailable, and Oddo, who

THE DREAM

was a slightly more accurate crosser than Cafu. I didn't want him to have to look after Ronaldo all by himself, so I asked Gattuso to keep an eye on him too.

By this stage we had settled on the Christmas Tree as our default formation, although it might be more accurate to call it a hybrid between a 4–4–1–1 out of possession and 4–3–2–1 in possession. We dominated from the start in driving rain at the San Siro. Because we needed to win, we pushed more from the outset. We were ahead after only 11 minutes, Kaká interchanging with Seedorf before finishing clinically from just outside the box. That was his third goal of the tie. United must have been sick of the sight of him. Ten minutes later Seedorf muscled his way past a couple of defenders to score from a similar distance. As the two players operating behind Inzaghi, they were different but perfectly complementary. Kaká was all speed and skill while Seedorf relied on strength and steel. Between them they were a total menace. In the second half I brought Gilardino off the bench and he removed all further doubt, running on to Ambrosini's pass from deep to make it 3–0 and complete a masterclass.

I have been a manager for more than 800 games in my career. If I had to choose the best two performances put on by any of my teams, one would be this semi-final against Manchester United. Watching your team play as we did in the first half was so good that I just sat back and enjoyed it, almost like a fan. I didn't need to do anything. In the first 45 minutes we played perfect football. Pirlo and Seedorf dictated the

THE FOURTH TIME, 2005–7

rhythm of the game and Kaká, being Kaká, was just magical. But Gattuso was the man of the match. He was a beast and a demon as he followed Ronaldo everywhere to stop him having any real influence. How Gattuso lasted until 80 minutes before he was booked is a mystery but, as soon as he was, I substituted him for Cafu. Naturally, it was Scholes, another fighter, with whom he had the trouble. As Gattuso left the field, his emotions boiled over. He began encouraging the crowd to show their approval for our performance. The crowd responded. Perhaps this was regrettable, but at this level of the competition such things happen.

After the game my good friend Alex Ferguson told me that our performance was one of the best in Milan's history. While he wished us the best of luck for the final, he added that we wouldn't need it. I gave him my best bottle of wine and he said that he would only drink it when he saw me lift the trophy.

Incredibly, Milan were back in the final for the third time in five years. It was an achievement for us to be proud of, especially in the light of everything going on that season. But there was a twist. Also back in the final for the second time in three years were Liverpool, who beat José Mourinho's Chelsea on penalties in the other semi-final. Having met in Istanbul, this time we would need to cross the Aegean to meet again in Athens. We had been desperate for them to beat Chelsea so that we could right the wrongs of the so-called 'miracle in Istanbul'. Revenge was certainly uppermost

THE DREAM

in the mind of our president. 'We are going to Athens to take back from Liverpool the cup they took from our hands two years ago,' he said. 'Two years ago, we lost an incredible game but this time we will be ready for anything.'

In some respects, Liverpool were a stronger side than the one that beat us on penalties two years earlier. Benitez had bolstered their midfield with the purchases of Javier Mascherano, and they had Bolo Zenden on the left. Dudek was on the bench, like Hyppiä, while Pepe Reina had the number one jersey. Instead of Baroś up front they had the hard-running Dirk Kuyt. Their style of play was more physical than Manchester United's. And they were well organised defensively. But I wasn't worried. Despite those nightmare six minutes in Istanbul, we had proved that we knew how to play in games of this magnitude, and we never really had a bad game at this level. And even though this was the end of a long season, the squad was in a better physical condition than we had been in Istanbul. The Christmas break had done the trick and worked its magic.

It was great news that Maldini, who had been struggling with a knee injury, was available at the last minute. The following month he would turn 39, but his wisdom and experience still made him indispensable. My one worry was Inzaghi's hamstrings. He was an extraordinary striker, and I felt a strong bond with him. Strikers are more complex than other players because of the nature of the job they do. They can be arrogant and simultaneously fragile. It just depends on whether or not they're scoring. Inzaghi was no different. Kaká was our top goalscorer in Europe that season, but Inzaghi had netted a few too. And he lived for European games.

If he was ready, I really wanted to pick him. It was a case of him or Gilardino. A clinical finisher or a player who thrives on fast counter-attacks and one-on-ones? The other choice of Ronaldo, who had been doing well in Serie A, was not open to me as he was cup-tied. Everyone at the club and in the media assumed I would not take the risk with Inzaghi, even though he'd worked hard to get into condition. The assumption was that I'd start with Gilardino and make the switch if the need arose.

It had not been Inzaghi's best season for us, and he'd allowed a mistake or two to creep into his game. That is understandable. When you don't play much, the pressure can get to you. I remember our general manager, Galliani, watching our last training session before the final. Inzaghi could barely trap a ball. He didn't look ready for such a big responsibility.

'Why don't we let Gilardino play?' Galliani said. 'He looks to be in much better shape than Inzaghi.'

But I had a sixth sense. After 30 years in the game, I'd developed an eye, and I'd learned to trust it. He had the added motivation that, alone among his team-mates, he had not been fit to play in Istanbul.

'Inzaghi is a strange animal,' I replied. 'Maybe tomorrow will be his night.'

THE DREAM

The following night I sent out seven players who had started in Istanbul. Dida, Nesta, Maldini, Pirlo, Gattuso, Seedorf, Kaká. Plus Inzaghi. My family of players who had been together for so long. Oddo and Jankulovski were at fullback. Ambrosini played in central midfield. Together they had a collective memory that they wanted to erase as a team. As only three of them were still in their twenties, they knew that this was probably their last chance to win the Champions League together.

Inzaghi did not prove me wrong. As half-time approached Kaká won a free kick on the edge of the box. Pirlo and Seedorf lined up over the ball and Inzaghi attached himself to the right-hand end of the wall. What happened next looked like a fluke, and perhaps it was, but if so, it was a calculated fluke. As Pirlo drilled his shot past the edge of the wall, Inzaghi peeled back to let it through. The ball clipped his chest and carried on towards the goal. Reina had already committed to diving the other way. Did Inzaghi deliberately plan for the ball to touch him? Or did he get lucky and happen to be in the way? The answer is it's probably a bit of both. He had certainly scored goals like that before, and claimed it was based on his knowledge of Pirlo's free-kick technique.

As the game wore on, Liverpool became more desperate and with 12 minutes to go Benitez played his Peter Crouch card – bringing on a tall focal point for direct back-to-front play. I sent on Kaladze, not for Crouch specifically, but to bolster up the defence generally and protect our lead.

THE FOURTH TIME, 2005–7

Instead, we doubled it with a stereotypical Inzaghi goal in the 82nd minute. Kaká picked up the ball on the right with no Liverpool player anywhere near him. He had plenty of time to size up his options and slipped the ball into space through the heart of the defence. Jamie Carragher disastrously chose to step up to catch Inzaghi offside. Big mistake. Carragher had forgotten Ferguson's joke about Inzaghi being born offside. Inzaghi, hanging on his shoulder, skipped into the box, pushed the ball round Reina and put the game beyond doubt.

There were eight minutes left. Liverpool needed only six minutes to score three in Istanbul so you could never be certain. I took Inzaghi off in the 88th minute and brought on Gilardino to enjoy a taste of the final. Kuyt immediately headed in a corner and dashed back to the centre spot with the ball. In his own words, Inzaghi spent the remaining minutes 'marking the linesman' as he waited to see if his two goals would be cancelled out. But there was no miracle in Athens. Not for Liverpool. We had our revenge. The bill had been paid, we could move on.

It was a very special victory. At the turn of the year I had been under mounting pressure, although I regarded all that stuff in the media as external noise. It was a difficult time because the players were tired and had lost some confidence. It was my job to regrow that confidence, and fortunately I did my job. We worked hard to make things better.

But another thing was the team itself. When I look back at our line-up for that game it is difficult to imagine anyone

THE DREAM

better to fill any of the positions. Every piece was selected to complement and enhance the whole. Every player was the perfect fit because the system was designed to fit them, not the other way round. The amazing thing is that it was one of the oldest teams ever to win the Champions League. Only three players were in their twenties. The average age was 31. It just goes to prove that sometimes age is just a number. You're never too old! Our youngest player, Kaká, was the top scorer in the competition and went on to win the Ballon d'Or that year. What a season.

And then there was the background. I did not see this victory as revenge for the *Calciopoli* scandal, and yet this was an important moment for the whole of Italian football. We were able to get back some of our credibility in world football.

We were all emotional at the final whistle. Inzaghi most of all. As the team celebrated in front of banks of photographers, Maldini and I had a special moment together. He put his arm around me and, even if we didn't say anything, maybe we had the same thought running through our heads: that this was the fourth time we had been here together with Milan. It was also to be the last.

Two days after lifting the trophy, Paulo had an operation on his knee. When he woke up from the anaesthetic, he kept asking whether we had won or lost. Maybe we had done more than that. After *Calciopoli*, maybe we had redeemed the credibility of Italian football in the eyes of Europe and the world.

I never did ask Sir Alex if he enjoyed that bottle of wine.

THE FOURTH TIME, 2005–7

At AC Milan, Paolo Maldini was a team-mate of Carlo for two successful European Cups and was managed by Carlo for two more Champions League wins.

I knew of Carlo before he came to Milan because my father, Cesare, coached him at Parma and used to play him as a number nine or ten, so he was a top scorer for that team. My father and Nils Liedholm, who was very influential for Carlo, played together in the great Milan team of the late 1950s.

Liedholm was this mythic figure in football in Italy. He coached both Carlo at Roma and gave me my debut at Milan. The big lesson that Carlo took from him was that he didn't look at you to see whether you're a big name or if you just came up from the academy, but he looked just at what you did on the pitch; if he thought you were ready then he would play you. He gave you the confidence just to go onto the pitch and be your best self and try new things. He was a visionary and, for players with talent, the best coach ever. Carlo is in that same mould.

I was very young when Carlo came to Milan as a player. When you're 18 you're not much involved in questioning how good or bad an incoming player is or is not, but all the other players thought that Carlo could be a great signing. Although we had a very great back line, we needed some higher-level players with creativity and energy in the midfield. But there was a concern. Carlo was coming back

THE DREAM

from a very bad injury and in the beginning he suffered a little bit.

From the start a small group of us started speaking and drinking and integrating a lot. The discussions were like a magic potion, a superpower – we were like kids, but we were living a dream. Carlo knew the dream too because he had experience of a European Cup final where he didn't play. You think that this will happen just once in your life. So to get to the final we thought Carlo could help us with this and, of course, that is why Sacchi chased him.

Although we began thinking about winning the cup from early on, the earlier rounds had a different structure in those days so we were working out how to get to the final. Although there were fewer games it was very tricky because if you had a bad game you were out.

Sacchi's tactics never changed but what he did do was to change our mindset for the European Cup. He gave us a feeling that in the biggest games we would win. He gave us his confidence and Carlo understood from Sacchi that giving confidence is a coach's most important role. Both were criticised for not winning more Scudetti but Serie A was the toughest league in the 1980s and early 1990s. There was Napoli with Maradona, Sampdoria with Mancini and Vialli, and we shared a stadium with Inter, who had Matthäus and Klinsmann. My God, it was tough. It was not enough to be the best. You had to have some luck also.

THE FOURTH TIME, 2005–7

Take our first game against Red Star. Basically, we were out. There was no chance for us to score. If it hadn't been for the fog, there would have been no European Cup that first year. We remember the fog but also the Donadoni injury. It was a bad challenge, and Roberto turned blue. We were traumatised, we were all crying, but then there was something said on the public address and one of the Red Star players translated, telling me that Roberto was OK. There's no way of winning a game like that if in your mind you cannot focus on the pitch.

Later in that campaign we came up against Real Madrid and that was something special: 5–0. It was important because Madrid was the benchmark for Berlusconi – that's who he wanted us to be compared with. We were new in the way we were playing, and I don't think they were organised to play against us. But believe me, we had great athletes in that team. The way we used to train and work hard was unusual for football at that time. I was a beast at that age, but on Friday I would say, 'I cannot play, I'm dead, I'm dead.' Sacchi's training was the hardest, but Carlo kept up even though it must have been hard for him. He knew when his body was not in the perfect place to play but he was great, never complained, always available, and he played on the wing when he was put there. He was a great model for us younger players.

Our first final was against Steaua Bucharest in Barcelona. We won 4–0. That was incredible. It was all Milan fans. No one was allowed to come up from Romania, against 90,000 people coming from Milan. So, to get there for us was, I mean, goose pimples, but for them probably it was, 'We're done, we're done.' It was impossible for them to win, impossible. They were a very good team, but we had everything going for us.

Next year was the Benfica final. It was more normal for us there even though it was a very difficult final, you know, against Eriksson, who was their coach, but it was a pretty smooth way of getting there and winning there. That was a result of the experience of the year before. We were now used to it – you've achieved the dream, in one sense, and knew it could be achieved. When I played my first game as a senior player I say, now I know I can play. I belong here. That also happens when you reach a kind of result – we can beat champions, we can win the Champions League. My first game – win the game, then win the league, then the European Cup, then anything. The culture has changed, we are champions now.

It runs through the whole club – it leads to excellence not only on the pitch but in the changing room. So, everything from Milanello, the chef, waiters, how you dress – you know, the first two years with Berlusconi. For example, the club would provide a tutor to teach players how to read a newspaper, how to read in other languages, how to behave with other people or when meeting with someone. So, every single day the president was bringing us someone to teach us something, between the training sessions.

You train in the morning, you go to recover, then you have training in the afternoon. So, in the afternoon when it's summer usually you train at 5.30, 5, 6pm, to sleep because you are dead and it was, 'Guys, you have to go for education.' At first it was terrible for us but then you start thinking, 'Wow, he did it for a purpose.' So now we have more knowledge I'd say on everything. All so that the environment was ready to win. And the different nationalities added to the culture. And Carlo was watching and learning from this.

But as with us all, he came to his final game, and we have good and funny memories of that game. The last game for Carlo as a player was against Verona. He was on the bench; it was the last game of the season and we'd won the league already. We were tied at 0–0 and had used two of the three substitutes permitted. Then Capello turned to the bench, and he said to [Aldo] Serena, 'Go in', and Carlo was sitting there, and Aldo looked at Capello and shook his finger and said, 'No, it is for Carlo.' Capello was not happy to be resisted but he finally agreed and turned to Carlo – 'Carlo, go in.' Carlo ran on and with his first touch decided to show off with a couple of stepovers, a move he loved to do when he was young, but the pitch wasn't good in Milan, and he tripped himself up and he fell on his face – boom – and we were all laughing, shit, Carlo's last game, he leaves us like

THE DREAM

this . . . but then he scored two goals. He only tells the story about the goals.

Nine years later Carlo returned to Milan, this time as the Mister and I was the player. He had learned good and bad lessons at Reggiana, Parma and Juventus. The first thing he did was to give me the responsibility of managing the locker room and playing, and he would focus on other stuff. Of course, he was macro-managing the locker room, but he gave me credit. He allowed me to lead, to do the sort of job that Carlo himself did when he was a player for Sacchi, to be his guy on the pitch. He allowed me to do it my way. I think that you can learn, because you know, I learned from many coaches, from many men, but then I have to decide what to keep and what to discard and Carlo encouraged that learning. He had learned himself from Sacchi, from Liedholm and then he added the final pieces from Carlo. I did the same. It was unspoken but our relationship had to change. So, he gave me responsibilities, but he was the coach, I was the player – we cannot just be friends. We were friends – I used to call him Carlo, not Coach, and he used to call me Paolo, but the separation had to be clear. The other players had to know that there were no favourites. It worked for us both. I was able to be me personally, my best moment. Not only as a player but also in my life. I was still immature, and Carlo was the best coach ever for me in that period of my life. So, from day one I enjoyed playing football because before it was *only work but with Carlo I also enjoyed life, football and experiences, from day one to the last day of my career.*

As a coach Carlo was the father of the team, and I was the eldest son. Eventually we both had to leave. It was very nice because we left there the same day. It was sad for me, sad for him, but I enjoyed so much those years from 2001 to 2009. We had a group of people that really had fun together. He called me the day after I quit to go to Chelsea, but it was too soon. I did go to speak with Abramovich, but it was to say, 'I'm not ready for this.'

What makes Carlo special is that his decades of experience make him among the best in terms of knowledge of the game. For example, as a player he would have learned from other managers; from Sacchi, the discipline, the work ethic, how to deal with (or not) big players. Sacchi maybe did not handle the Dutch players so well because they did not fit into the culture as Sacchi wanted. But Carlo learned from that. He saw that they [the Dutch] brought new ideas as well as some problems and those new ideas were valuable. They had to be understood as men not just players and Carlo is great at that. But Carlo also understood what Sacchi brought. Capello was the opposite of Carlo, but he learned from Capello also.

Where Carlo differs from some other coaches is that for Carlo, it's not about being remembered as the best coach ever, a coach that changed the world. He wants to be Carlo Ancelotti, a winner, and he can win giving credit to everyone

THE DREAM

because he always says that thanks to this, thanks to Real Madrid, it's not just a way of saying – he means it, it's the truth. Some coaches want to be the one that determines the result but in the end the players do – and Carlo knows that. Football is not an individual sport, so that also brings you an idea of winning a victory so you can share it with your people – everyone is important, is involved and credit must go to Mr Berlusconi for bringing a culture of excellence to the club. Carlo flourished in that environment both as a player and as a coach/manager.

Also, perhaps the title 'manager' suits him better than coach because he sees the job as coaching by teaching to be a man. So, if as a man with a strong identity, with good values, Carlo will bring you to a level where you're responsible for yourself, and that's something with which players can relate. Top players respond to being trusted. Tactically, he sees things, like playing someone like Pirlo in a different position so that he can use his skills for the benefit of the team. For me, he deserves the best because of what he has represented, how he developed in his life and career. He is one of the best, for me, in the world of sport. If he's happy I'm more happy than him, so for me, I believe that luck goes where it needs to go, so he deserves it – that's Carlo.

11

BLUE IS THE COLOUR, 2007–11

I've never been sure how long a coach should stay at one club. Some get their best results in the first season and have lost the squad by the third. I had now been at Milan for a long time, and the truth is that I did once consider leaving for a fresh challenge when Real Madrid made an approach in 2006 and I was ready to accept the offer.

'We want you. You're the best,' said the club officials when I met them. This was at the time when Milan were taking on Barcelona in the semi-final of the Champions League. Even so, it wasn't a difficult decision. The money was very good and I was ready to sign a preliminary contract. However, before I did, I insisted on the insertion of a clause: 'This contract will become valid only once AC Milan gives its consent.' In other words, I would leave Milan only if they wanted me to. I was very open with Galliani about this opportunity, and he urged me to stay, and offered me a contract extension, so I signed.

By that time, I was the longest-surviving coach at any club in Serie A. If I stayed until 2008 I would become the

THE DREAM

longest-serving coach over a single spell in Milan's history. (The history books record that Nereo Rocco had control of more matches, but over two separate periods.)

The next season we won the Champions League. But the season after, in 2007–8, we had a terrible hangover. Our ageing squad kept going, with only Costacurta finally choosing to end his career. If there was a lesson that season, it was in the need to stock up on fresh blood when the going was good. We didn't quite manage this. The main addition to the pool of talent was Alexandre Pato, who arrived as an exciting striker from Brazil, still in his teens.

That season brought the odd ray of sunshine. In December, for the first time we won the Club World Cup, beating Boca Juniors in Japan. But our domestic season in Serie A was a disaster. We started as badly as we had a year earlier, and didn't manage to win at home until halfway through January.

Our only hope of salvation was once again in the Champions League. We qualified for the round of 16, yet again finishing top of a group that also included Celtic, Benfica and Shakhtar Donetsk. Our opponents were Arsenal. This was billed as a clash of youth and experience. The average age of our team was over 30, while theirs was not much more than 25.

I don't actually think age came into it in the away leg. We were not outrun or outpaced. But this doesn't mean the players were not mentally tired from the previous season and from their long time in the game and from their many seasons experiencing the relentless pressure that comes with representing the Rossoneri.

We started to drop deep and let them have many more chances as the game went on. That we managed to hold them to a goalless draw was thanks in part to our reserve keeper, the Australian Zeljko Kalac, who came into the side that season as Dida was suffering from injury and a loss of form. Kalac was named man of the match. They had a chance to win it in the dying seconds but Emmanuel Adebayor saw his header from close range bounce off the bar.

That should have given us encouragement for Arsenal's trip to the San Siro. But we were not able to be penetrative. Their energy levels remained high even at the end of the game while ours flagged. On 84 minutes Cesc Fàbregas received the ball in the centre circle, drove forward, managed to brush past Gattuso and from 30 yards drilled a low shot that bounced once before going just inside the left-hand post. That goal killed us off, since we then needed two goals. In injury time Arsenal tapped in a second instead. We had to be honest and accept that we were clearly second best to a side who took control of the game, pressed without let-up and dominated us.

With Milan I had been to three finals of the Champions League, winning it twice, as well as a semi-final and a quarter-final. To be eliminated before the quarter-finals was

THE DREAM

my worst finish in the competition since Juventus failed to get out of their group in 2000. Some of the squad found it very difficult to get used to such a scenario. Kakà was not used to failure and was clearly shocked.

'It happens – that's football,' I said to him. 'Acknowledge it, but never accept it.'

Whether others would acknowledge it was out of my hands. That season we eventually had a run of decent results in Serie A but it was not enough to get us into the qualifying places for next season's Champions League. So for the first time since I arrived at Parma 12 years earlier, I would not be sending out a side to take part in Europe's top competition.

When you go down a level in Europe, you find yourself playing in all sorts of interesting places. The following season – 2008–9 – the UEFA Cup took us to Zürich, Heerenveen and an extremely old-school stadium in Portsmouth. In the round of 32 we were knocked out on away goals by German club Werder Bremen. In the league we achieved the basic target of qualifying for the Champions League for the following season, although Berlusconi was unhappy that we didn't win the Scudetto. He even took time off from his duties as prime minister of Italy to say so in public.

As the older players started to retire or move on, the San Siro was an interesting place to be for anyone who liked to see the names of *galácticos* on the team sheet. Who should turn up over the course of the season but Ronaldinho and

BLUE IS THE COLOUR, 2007–11

David Beckham. Beckham came on loan from LA Galaxy in the United States in search of playing time before the Euros. I felt honoured that Capello, then the England manager, had advised him that I would take good care of him. Gianluca Zambrotta, formerly of Juventus, arrived after two years at Barcelona and started more games than anyone in the squad. And we were pleased to welcome Shevchenko back from Chelsea, where he wasn't being used, although he did not have such a successful stay this time. None of these names did much to bring down the average age of the squad.

Since the previous season, when we were knocked out by Arsenal, the media had been talking about a great era in the club's history having come to an end. If I'm honest, that's how it felt to me too. Very few coaches can stay in one job and keep refreshing the squad and winning at the same time. I had enjoyed more success than I could have imagined with Milan. I had realised the dream of Champions League triumph twice. But I now started to understand that the moment had arrived for the club and me to go our separate ways a year earlier than my contract stipulated. And when I mentioned it to the club and told them that there was interest from another club with big ambitions, they agreed that it was probably time. They were very graceful about it, and showed me total respect.

Maldini and I were the last link with the great Sacchi experiment, which had brought two European Cups. We would go out of the door together. He was 40. I was about to be 50. It was time for both of us to try something new. In the dressing room after our final farewell to the Milan fans in the San Siro, I don't mind admitting that there were tears. It's difficult to say goodbye to your family. I did ask Maldini to come with me to London as my assistant, but, after so many years of playing, he needed to put his feet up and he said no.

My first conversations with Chelsea had taken place at the end of the previous season. The offer of a job looked likely until they decided on appointing Luiz Felipe Scolari. I heard it suggested that Roman Abramovich didn't think I spoke English well enough. Scolari didn't have a good time in the Premier League and left halfway through the season, to be replaced by Guus Hiddink as a temporary solution. Chelsea started talking to me again. Soon enough, rumours of a potential move leaked out into the press, the way these things do. Beckham revealed that I had been taking English lessons since before he arrived in the winter transfer window. What was unusual about the negotiations was that they did a lot of due diligence, trying to find out as much about me as they could before offering me the position. This led to a long succession of meetings where they asked me to discuss detailed strategies and objectives.

It was very different from my appointment to Milan, which was more of an overnight bank raid. The upshot was that in March 2009 I agreed in principle to join Chelsea.

BLUE IS THE COLOUR, 2007–11

After a very intense week of language lessons, I took up my post in June and was proud to give my first press conference in English. I even cracked my first joke in a foreign language. Someone asked about the importance of John Terry, as there was some doubt about whether he would stay. I described him as the symbol of the team but said that I didn't know if he would be captain next season. This was greeted by a moment of silent astonishment.

'I like to joke at press conferences,' I explained.

Some of the directors started learning Italian, maybe to give me a helping hand, and I was pleased to have Ray Wilkins, who learned his Italian while at Milan, as my assistant. He became a good friend and, with his skill at translating, a valuable link with the squad. I discovered that Italian was useful in one respect. I couldn't get emotional in English, so if I wanted to raise my voice I did it in my own language. Then the players knew for sure I was angry.

The club made it worth my while. The basic salary was extremely generous and on top of it Abramovich offered a bonus if I could win the Champions League for Chelsea. There was no reason to suppose such a target was impossible. Under José Mourinho and the club's various successors, Chelsea had reached the semi-final five times in the past six seasons, and the final once, when they lost on penalties. It was a hell of a record. The squad that came so near so often was still together. I inherited the spine of a great side with a strong English flavour provided by John

Terry, Frank Lampard and Ashley Cole. Among the core of great players lining up alongside them were Petr Čech in goal, Michael Essien, Michael Ballack, Florent Malouda and Deco in midfield, Didier Drogba and Nicolas Anelka up front. The average age was quite high, and when you're trying to win the Champions League, experience on the pitch is important.

It helps too when you take charge of such an impressive group if you have a couple of Champions League victories on your CV. But I knew that my record would get me only so far. Abramovich made it clear that he wanted me to win it with Chelsea, and he also wanted Chelsea to carve out their own identity on the pitch. To meet that demand, I decided that we needed to play more possession football than was the style under Mourinho and his successors. In order to help achieve this I even tried to sign Pirlo, but that proved impossible. I also tried to sign Pato. In the end the only person who joined me from Milan was Bruno Demichelis from my backroom staff. Bruno was behind the Milan Lab that was credited with ensuring the longevity of players such as Maldini.

Very early on in the pre-season, we took part in a mini-league in the United States. At Pasadena, where, the last time I visited, I had been Sacchi's assistant coach in the World Cup final in 1994, Chelsea beat Inter, the Italian champions who were coached by Mourinho. Then we flew to Baltimore and I had the very strange experience of sending out a side to play *against* Milan, a team full of players who had been part of my family for years. (Kaká was not among them as he had now joined Real Madrid.) We won again. Against Milan there was a stunning long-distance strike from Drogba.

Things carried on going very well. In the Premier League we couldn't stop winning, even though it took me a while to find my preferred system. I started with Lampard at the tip of a diamond and Essien at its base, but the latter then got injured in the Africa Cup of Nations. Eventually we evolved into a kind of 4–3–3 with a lot of free-flowing movement. We got into the habit of beating the top sides – Liverpool, Arsenal, Manchester United. We got maximum points against all of them, home and away.

There was only one small bump in the road. In late September we went to Wigan and lost 3–1. This was when the first hint of a shadow fell across my time at the club. Abramovich was at the training ground the morning after, and he was demanding answers. What had gone wrong? The most obvious answer was that Čech was sent off early in the second half, just after Drogba had equalised. The truth is that they played well, and we didn't.

I had never had this level of surveillance from Berlusconi. Sure, he was a demanding owner to work for, sometimes buying players I didn't need and expecting me to fit them into the side, or arguing with me about tactics and selection. Maybe because for a lot of my time at the club Berlusconi was also the prime minister of Italy, there was no micromanagement. He had more important things to think about. Now I was working for a Russian oligarch who, I suddenly understood, expected everything to go well all the time. And if it didn't, he wanted to know why. It was my job to supply the answers. Soon we went to the top of the table and we stayed there until mid-March. As I say, very occasionally I would lose my temper and shout in Italian. This was partly something over which I had little control, but it was also a tactical ploy to electrify the squad and remind them who was the Mister.

Meanwhile in the Champions League we were drawn in a group with Porto, Atlético Madrid and the Cypriot club APOEL. We won our first three games, which I always knew was important, and easily topped the group. The most entertaining game was in Madrid, where Sergio Agüero scored for them on 66 minutes, Drogba got two back, only for Agüero to get another in injury time. It didn't matter, because we had already qualified.

The draw for the round of 16 pitted us against Inter. Maybe this was a trick of fate that was inevitably going to be played on me and my opposite number Mourinho. The tie meant that both of us would be going back to our old stadiums. For a season we had been rivals in Milan with teams who played in the San Siro – we had one home win apiece against each other in Serie A. Now I was going to send out a team that consisted of many players he knew well from his time at Chelsea. He had won two Premier League titles with them as well as other cups. If he needed any extra motivation to win, it was that the only time Chelsea had reached the Champions League final they did it without him, after Abramovich sacked him.

I tried to stay away from all the noise but there was always tension between us. It was mostly mind games generated by him, and although it never meant very much it was amplified by the media, who loved these knockabout subplots. One writer called it 'box office gold'. I admit that sometimes I did fan the flames. The day before the game I claimed that all Italy would want Chelsea to beat Inter. But then Mourinho had just earned himself a three-match ban from the touchline in Serie A.

We nearly held our own at the San Siro against a team that included Wesley Sneijder in midfield and Samuel Eto'o up front. But the problem for us in both legs was getting past their excellent Brazilian goalkeeper Júlio César and the very experienced defence lined up in front of him. Between them, the Argentinians Javier Zanetti and Walter Samuel and Lúcio from Brazil were as old and wily as any defence I selected for Milan. Meanwhile Chelsea were afflicted by injuries to first-choice defenders. At Stamford Bridge I was forced to select our third-choice keeper. And our best defender, John Terry, was having difficulties in his private life that meant the press were all over him.

THE DREAM

Diego Milito scored in the third minute in Milan. Then at a similar point in the second half Salomon Kalou stroked in an elegant shot through a crowded area, and we had our away goal. Four minutes later Inter's midfielder Esteban Cambiasso leapt on a half-clearance and hit a fierce drive into the far corner to make it 2–1.

That weekend there was a repeat of the Wigan post-mortem when, for the second time that season, we lost to Manchester City, which was managed by my old Azzurri team-mate Roberto Mancini. They beat us 4–2 at home and Abramovich made his now familiar demand for answers. This was not the easiest backdrop for our next home game, when we would try to reverse the deficit against Inter. It was tight, but we couldn't overcome their stout, last-ditch defending. With 11 minutes to go, Sneijder sent a searching chip forward for Eto'o to run on to and drive home.

The next day Abramovich didn't talk just to me but to the whole squad. Soon there were questions in the press that I might not be at Chelsea the following season. But I honestly didn't think the owner could have any real complaints. That season we scored more goals in the Premier League than any team in its history. Drogba got 29, Lampard 22. Our tally of 103 was six more than Manchester United in the 1999–2000 season, and 31 more than Mourinho's team got in both his title-winning seasons. Twice we scored seven in a single match and, on the last day at home to Wigan, we got eight. I was pleased with this because I don't consider myself

Competing with one of the greatest players ever.

A foggy night in Belgrade, 1988. We could hardly make out the players close to us.

My opening goal in our famous 5–0 defeat of Madrid in April 1989.

My first European Cup with teammates Baresi, Van Basten and Gullit.

Preparing to retain the Cup the following season.

Cup retained.

My first win as coach in 2003, after a final between two Italian teams.

Passing by the trophy that was snatched from us in 2005, during six minutes in Istanbul.

Istanbul avenged in 2007. Maldini and I celebrating together for the fourth and last time.

Cristiano puts us 4–0 in front of Bayern in the 90th minute – I can relax at last.

Relief after being so close to defeat in the 2014 final.

The joy of victory in my first season back at Real Madrid in 2022.

Madridistas sharing our victory in the streets of Madrid.

Victory celebrations on our return to the Bernabeu.

Elation at the final whistle against Dortmund in 2024.

Number seven in London. Winning that last cup felt as good as the first time.

an especially attacking coach. I have the defensive mindset of an Italian coach and came from a Serie A tradition where the Scudetto is won not by scoring most but conceding least. It proved I was capable of adapting. I brought my usual way of doing things with me: work hard on the training ground, but also keep things light-hearted. When I felt tense, of course I tried to shield the players and keep it to myself. And when there were problems, I encouraged the players to speak out.

There was something freeing about being in England. The stadiums were fuller than in Italy, they were more welcoming with much less violence in the stands. This sense of freedom was expressed on the pitch. When we were ahead, I encouraged the team to keep on scoring. That rarely happened in the safety-first environment of Serie A.

We won the League and then we won the FA Cup, beating Portsmouth in the final. The double was not as rare as it had once been in England. Since the creation of the Premier League, Manchester United had done it three times and Arsenal twice. All the same, it was a major achievement. Chelsea had never done it before, not with any previous coach, including Mourinho. But that season he did go one better at Inter, who won the treble. It's still the only time an Italian club has managed such a feat. My problem was that Mourinho's triumph was not great for my relationship with Abramovich, who had sacked him. I was supposed to be the antidote to Mourinho, calm and measured and able to revive the squad after the drama of Mourinho. According to Abramovich, Mourinho was supposed to be a spent force. In allowing Mourinho to disrupt the script, I had embarrassed the owner.

I think I did my job, and it was hardly my fault that José was so successful at Inter. I honestly think that Inter was a sort of spiritual home for him. Mixing passion and discipline with an ability to conjure up a culture of us-against-the-world, he was a natural successor to Helenio Herrera and Giovanni Trapattoni. As I would discover, Diego Simeone at Atlético Madrid is another great manager in that image.

In a press conference at Wembley, after we won the Double, I expressed the wish to stay for a while. Maybe even ten years if the conditions were right. But of course, this was conditional on maintaining a good relationship with the owner. The club did not buy big over the summer. Ballack, Deco and Joe Cole moved on. Even though the ageing senior players who remained were now a year older, that did not worry me, especially when we won six of our first seven games of the 2010–11 season. The seventh win was at home to Arsenal. The day before I had the sad duty of attending the funeral of my father, who had died at the age of 87. Naturally, it was a very sad time for me, but I also knew that he would have wanted me to give my best to my work, which is what I did.

The first sign that things were awry for me came in November, after we lost to Liverpool. Their goals were scored by their prodigy, Fernando Torres. That week,

BLUE IS THE COLOUR, 2007-11

without consulting me first, the club decided not to renew Ray Wilkins's contract. I was sad to lose him, as Chelsea was in his blood. They promoted the head of opposition scouting Michael Emenalo as his replacement, although he had still to complete the necessary coaching qualifications. At a press conference I was asked if things might be different at a more normal club. 'This is a normal club!' I insisted. It was intended as a joke, and the media laughed. In private I told my employers that I was happy working with Demichelis and Paul Clement, who had come from coaching within the club's academy set-up. I quickly forged a strong relationship with Paul, who would later follow me to PSG and Madrid.

Around this time the players grew unhappy, and their discontent seemed to show on the pitch. We immediately started dropping points and by the time the January transfer window came round we had sunk to fifth. The club decided to come good on a plan that had been in the works for a while: to break the English transfer record and buy Torres from Liverpool for £50 million. A week later Torres had to play for his new club against his old club. Liverpool came to Stamford Bridge, packed their defence, and won 1-0.

But at least by then we had already qualified for the knockout stage of the Champions League. As ever, success or failure in Europe is how I would be measured by Abramovich. The incentive to win was, if anything, even greater this year, because the final was to be held at Wembley. We were drawn in a group with Marseille, Spartak Moscow and the Slovak club MŠK Žilina, and won our first five games. The last game, which we lost, was away against Marseille, but we had already won the group. Then in the round of 16 we were drawn against FC Copenhagen. The tie was won in the first leg away, thanks to the speed and accuracy of Anelka, who scored both goals in a 2–0 victory. A boring 0–0 draw in the second leg further solidified our win. In the quarter-final we were drawn against Alex Ferguson's Manchester United. It was the third time I'd met him in the competition, each time with a different club. So far, the score was 1–1. I had lost to them with Juventus, beaten them with Milan.

The good news was that we had recently beaten them in the league. First they came to Stamford Bridge and scored a well-made winner in the first half. Michael Carrick sent a long cross-field ball to Giggs, who was advancing on the left. His sublime first touch controlled the ball and beat his marker, Bosingwa. His second touch was a pull-back for Rooney, who made no mistake with his finish.

The night before the second leg, Abramovich decided to warn the squad that if they didn't win the tie there would be changes. He then told me that if we lost, I should not bother coming back in the next day. I didn't think this was a very wise move. Even if he was joking, clearly, he was feeling the tension. Giggs was again our destroyer, this time cutting in from the right to set up Javier Hernández (also known as Chicharito) for a tap-in. Something needed to change. We needed to score twice, knowing that United had conceded only three goals in nine Champions League games that entire season. Unfortunately, it looked as if none of those goals were going to come from Torres, who was clearly suffering from a lack of confidence and felt the weight of his transfer fee hanging round his neck. He had yet to score a single goal for Chelsea. I knew about this problem from my time with other strikers. Inzaghi, Shevchenko and Crespo had all suffered similar periods of goal famine. I wanted to support him. If you believe in a player, you have to stick with them. He needed to have time to return to his best. But this was Chelsea and Abramovich, which meant that we didn't have the luxury of time.

So at half-time I made what I knew would not be a decision welcomed in the directors' box and took Torres off and replaced him with Drogba. He briefly gave us hope when, not long after Ramires was sent off, he chested down a searching chip from Essien, drove forward and scored. But our hopes were dashed within a minute when Park Ji-sung ran on to yet another clever feed from Giggs.

In the dressing room Abramovich made it very clear what this defeat meant. I was in shock when I shared a drink with Ferguson straight after. 'Just forget it,' he said. 'He can't get rid of you in the middle of the season.' A few weeks on he was kind enough to say publicly that to sack me would be 'an astonishing decision'.

What happened next was inevitable. It doesn't really matter what the exact cause was. Perhaps the owner was outraged that I had taken off Torres, who had cost him so much money, and replaced him with a more reliable source of goals. Torres was his personal decision and substituting him was a direct rebuke to the owner. Momentarily, I had forgotten that, ultimately, you can't beat the owner. After three months, and 903 minutes of playing time, he scored his first goal in a Chelsea shirt in a 3–0 win over West Ham as we clawed our way back in the Premier League. In early May we went to Old Trafford. If we won that and our last two games, we would be champions. We lost it, then drew, then lost at Everton. I was honest with myself and with the press that I knew the axe might fall. Now it was just a question of how, and when. It came after I had given my post-match press conference. The CEO was leaving the stadium when he was told to turn round, get back to Goodison Park – and fire me.

On the bus back to London, the players had heard the news, and they were very kind. Ashley Cole said to me that we must all go out. I said that I couldn't because I had ten friends visiting from Italy who were coming round to my house for dinner.

'No, no, they must all come,' said Cole. 'I will send you a bus.'

So he sent a minibus to get me and my guests. The senior players – Cole, Terry, Lampard and Drogba – took me out to say goodbye. It was an unforgettable evening.

Manchester United made it to Wembley but were made to look second best by Pep Guardiola's Barcelona. Their eleven contained six of the players who played for Spain when they won the World Cup less than a year earlier. They also had Messi.

For the second time in my career, it was the Champions League that cost me my job. I didn't manage to fulfil the dream at Juventus and left after two seasons. I did at Milan and stayed for eight. I didn't at Chelsea, and after two I was on my way again.

I never spoke to Abramovich. In the week of my removal, I went to an awards dinner hosted by the League Managers Association. It was a pleasant evening. The manner of my sacking did not please the head of the organisation, Richard Bevan. 'It's damaging to the game,' he said. 'It's disrespectful to the Premier League and I think Mr Abramovich needs to have a long hard look at the advisors who he's got advising him. It's just a very poor way of running [a club]. He needs to have a little bit more respect for the history and tradition and culture.'

Well, perhaps Abramovich was right to let me go, because the following season Chelsea finally gave him the gift of a Champions League title – although he did fire my successor six months after he got his hands on the trophy.

As for me, I remember every day that I was at Chelsea as a good day.

12

JE NE REGRETTE RIEN, 2011–13

In Italy we have a saying: *Chiusa una porta, si apre un portone* (if one door closes, find a bigger door). After I left Stamford Bridge, I had only one question. Where to now? I was in limbo. The last time that had happened was after I left Parma in 1998. Back then I was soon approached by Juventus and asked to be the eventual replacement for Marcello Lippi when he left the club. This time it was different.

I was contracted to Chelsea for another season, and now I was free to put my feet up. I did think about staying on in England. In fact, in my severance negotiations, I made sure that a clause in my contract – one denying me the opportunity to go straight on to another Premier League club – was removed. My name was even linked in the media to an English club or two, as well as to my old club Roma. I certainly stuck around in England that autumn, wondering if a job at one of the bigger clubs might come free. But I was in no hurry. I wasn't afraid of taking a year out. For now at least, there would be no dreaming of another Champions League campaign. Maybe I needed some time off from meeting the demands of ambitious and super-wealthy owners.

Then I got a call from Qatar Sports Investments or, to be more precise, the person on the other end of the line was Leonardo. I knew him well. The Brazilian ex-international was technical director towards the end of my time at Milan, and he took over from me as coach after I left in 2009. His relationship with Berlusconi didn't go well, and he only lasted a season. Unusually he then moved straight across to Inter, again staying no longer than a season. He resigned in the summer of 2011 to take up a post as sporting director at Paris Saint-Germain.

This was around the time the club was purchased by Qatar Sports Investments. Overnight, PSG became one of the richest clubs in the world. With wealth came ambition. Like all such presidents, Nasser Al-Khelaifi wanted the club to win Europe's top prize. But PSG hadn't even won Ligue 1 since the early 1990s, and in the 2010–11 season the club had not managed to qualify for the following season's Champions League. In the 2011–12 season, they got knocked out of the Europa League in the group stage. So the club was not in great shape.

Paris is a strange football city. Some of the biggest ideas in football have come out of France. The World Cup was the brainchild of Jules Rimet, a Frenchman. The European Cup was conceived in a Paris hotel. The Ballon d'Or

JE NE REGRETTE RIEN, 2011–13

is the creation of a French football magazine. But for some reason the capital of France has only one top football club. In London, I had ten derby games a season against other London clubs. The ground of the nearest rivals, Fulham, was within walking distance of Stamford Bridge. The closest PSG had to a local rival was Lille. I'm not qualified to say whether this lack of local rivals was a factor, but a big club in a big European city was surely meant to be doing better.

In December 2011, even though the club was going well in Ligue 1, the new owners decided to sack the previous coach. The idea was to replace him with a bigger name and a proven record of winning things. Leonardo came to me and asked if I would consider a move to Paris. There was none of the extended courtship and intense interrogation that had characterised the approach from Chelsea, and it was nice to be asked. At first it was pleasant to have four months not even speaking about football, but when the English and Italian leagues started, I began to get a bit restless. I was tired of not working. So I agreed to a two-and-a-half-year contract.

It was soon clear that the new owners hadn't had time to put the club on a well-organised footing. My first act was to ask Paul Clement to join me as my assistant. I made many other changes over that season that were all designed to turn PSG into the sort of club that, from top to bottom, felt like a potential challenger for the Champions League. I was able to draw on the knowledge of the great French midfielder

THE DREAM

Claude Makélélé, who had just retired in his late thirties. I didn't know him before I arrived but because he had been at Chelsea before me, I felt we understood each other, and he was able to advise me.

The moment I arrived at PSG I was bombarded by agents offering me the chance to buy players they represented, even ones who had only just signed contracts with other clubs. They were attracted by the city of Paris, the Qatari money and the prospect of working with a good coach. But I didn't go on a mad spending spree. I had inherited some good players who had only just arrived themselves, including Blaise Matuidi in midfield, Javier Pastore up front and, in goal, the Sicilian keeper Salvatore Sirigu. My first signings in the winter break included two Brazilians: Alex, the centre back I knew from Chelsea, and the left back Maxwell. I spent more money on the central midfielder Thiago Motta, who came from Inter. On the pitch, I bedded myself in with a friendly against Milan in Dubai. We went on to finish second in Ligue 1 and so qualified to re-enter Europe's top tier at the start of 2012–13.

The biggest boost to our ambitions was the arrival of Zlatan Ibrahimović in the close season of 2012. As if he wasn't famous enough already, his name was even bigger in France after that summer's Euros, when he scored for Sweden with a spectacular volley against Les Bleus. I discovered a player who was so hungry for goals that he would chase the last pass in the last minute in a training session in July if he thought he could get the goal that won the eight-a-side. For PSG that

JE NE REGRETTE RIEN, 2011–13

season he would score 30 goals. Also, in came Thiago Silva, whom I made captain. He was just as important a figure as Ibrahimović. He had the calm authority that reminded me of Franco Baresi. The pair of them set an inspirational example to the rest of the squad, two leaders who truly knew how to show others the way. The biggest fee the club paid was actually for Lucas Moura, the wide midfielder who arrived from Brazil and broke PSG's transfer record. From Napoli I also signed the lively Argentine striker Ezequiel Lavezzi.

That was a very positive influx of talent. Then in the winter transfer window, a year after we first tried to get him, we pulled a rabbit out of the hat and signed another great professional: none other than David Beckham. He wasn't just there to sell shirts. By then we were already top of the league and with his help we stayed there for the rest of the season, which PSG won for the first time in 19 years. It was a satisfying achievement to win a third league title in three different countries.

But the owners had made their feelings clear. They only had eyes for the Champions League. We did well in our group, beating Dynamo Kyiv and Dinamo Zagreb at home and away. But in our second game we lost away to Porto with a brilliant finish by James Rodríguez in the last ten minutes. That seemed to annoy my employers. The final game brought Porto to the Parc des Princes. Three days earlier we had lost in the league to Nice and to my great surprise the president and Leonardo threatened me with the sack if we did not beat

Porto. It didn't seem to matter that we had already qualified. They said it again the day before the match.

'We are following the project, not only the result,' they said, 'and we're not happy. We've decided that if we don't win this game, you will be sacked.'

To me this was ridiculous. Why on earth would they think that threatening the coach with the sack would help our progress? It just introduced a sense of instability and mistrust. So I decided there and then that I would leave at the end of the season irrespective of what might happen for the rest of it. I told Leonardo as much. If that was how they showed their faith in me, then I didn't want to stay, even if we went on to win the Champions League. We beat Porto 2–1. Thiago Silva led from the front with a powerful header. We quickly lost the lead but reclaimed it with a goal on the hour from Lavezzi. So I wasn't sacked, but I wasn't happy either and my mind was made up.

In the round of 16 we beat Valencia 2–1 away, even though Ibrahimović got himself sent off. Back in Paris it was a bit of a struggle. Valencia scored in the second half, and I started to worry that the tie was wide open again. If they got another they would win. But it woke us up, I changed the midfield to add more energy, and it worked. Lavezzi managed to pull one back in the 66th minute. Paris Saint-Germain would play in a quarter-final of the Champions League for the first time in 18 years.

The task of getting to the semi-final was formidable. We would have to beat Barcelona. After my time at PSG, the owners would try to solve the riddle of winning the Champions League by buying up *galácticos* as if they were collecting footballers for a Panini sticker album. For now, most of the big names – Messi, Xavi, Iniesta, Busquets, Villa, Fàbregas, Piqué, Alves – were on the opposition's team sheet, not ours.

I had been this far in the competition many times, so a quarter-final was nothing new to me. But this was the biggest tie that PSG had been involved in for years. They'd reached the semi-final in 1995. Other than that, their record in European competition was a virtual blank. So I was proud that in both legs we were able to show the world – and our success-hungry owners – that we could live with the best.

In the home game I decided not simply to contain Barcelona but to flood the side with attacking players. A lot of people were surprised that I selected Beckham to play in the Champions League for the first time in three seasons. He was now 37, and at the end of the season he would retire after an extraordinary career. But I needed his experience and his good footballing brain. I played him alongside Matuidi as part of a deep-sitting pair in central midfield to keep an eye on Xavi and Iniesta. They played incredibly well. While Matuidi surged forward, Beckham launched passes from deep to create counter-attacks for a quartet of quick players ahead of him: Lavezzi and Ibrahimović in the middle, Moura and Pastore coming in from wide. It was an ambitious plan.

We went behind when Messi was cleverly put in on the left and scored. Ibrahimović equalised after Thiago's header came back off the post. I would have been happy with that result but with only a minute to go Xavi put them ahead again from the spot. Then deep into extra time Matuidi put us back on terms with a deflected shot that deceived their keeper, Victor Valdés.

So Barcelona had two away goals. Unfortunately, the second of them would turn out to be crucial. At the Nou Camp there was reason to be hopeful because they had no Messi, who was injured. But he was on the bench, just in case he might be needed. We traded blows in the first half, which ended goalless. Early in the second a lovely throughball from Ibrahimović released Pastore, who put us up in the tie. We deserved our lead and now all we had to do was hold on for 40 minutes. We managed 20. By then Messi had come on with a brief to prise us open. I always joked that it's not fair to be able to introduce Messi when things are not going well for you. As only he could do, he teed up a move that you just can't defend against. The ball travelled in a quick, cleverly constructed triangle from him to David Villa to Pedro, whose shot was unstoppable. The tie finished 3–3. It was an honourable draw, but thanks to those two late goals in Paris, Barca were the ones who went through.

For the next three seasons PSG reached the quarter-finals, consolidating their reputation as a significant club in European football. But then the three after that it was just the round of 16. In 2020 they eventually made it to

JE NE REGRETTE RIEN, 2011–13

a final, still led by Thiago Silva, only to lose. Their solution after that was to augment their forward line, which already contained Kylian Mbappé, Neymar and Ángel Di María, by acquiring Messi. But at the time of writing, they are nearly there, and without the *galácticos*. It just goes to show. Money can't buy you love, and it can't always buy you silverware either.

After working for owners who wanted it all at Milan and Chelsea and Paris Saint-Germain, I thought I'd seen it all when it comes to presidential expectation.

Then I got a call from Real Madrid.

Luka Modrić has spent 12 years at Real Madrid and won three of his six Champions League titles under Ancelotti:

I came to Madrid in 2012 from Spurs with Mourinho as manager. So, before Carlo arrived, I had one year with José and before that I was with Harry Redknapp at Spurs and before that with Dinamo Zagreb. At Dinamo we only played qualifications for the Champions League, but we never reached the Champions League itself because it was more difficult then as you had to be league champions to qualify. I did manage to get there with Spurs, and we beat Inter Milan and Werder Bremen who, at the time, had a great team and great players. We got as far as the quarter-finals where we lost to – Real Madrid. The next season, although we finished fourth, we

THE DREAM

didn't qualify, as Chelsea were the holders and so they took our fourth spot. Harry was a great coach. I so much enjoyed playing under him. We played beautiful football under him. We played so good but the rest of the teams were really strong, but we played so, so good – such good football and we had very good players.

But it was different at Madrid. You feel it straight away when you arrive. When I arrived in 2012, Madrid was 12 years without winning the Champions League, and they were obsessed with La Décima. When I arrived they were all talking, 'All that matters for us is to win La Décima, no matter how,' and yes, you feel that this competition for Madrid is really special and it's – you know that you cannot win it all the time, but it's like an obligation for us at Madrid, and it's huge pressure because it's the competition that Madrid wants the most.

Mourinho for me was unlucky because he had three semi-finals and could not progress. But I am grateful because he was the one who brought me to Madrid. I only played one year with Mourinho, and we lost against Dortmund in the semi-final. I played and we lost 4–1 at Dortmund and beat them 2–0 at the Bernabéu. We were one goal away from going through. We missed so many chances and unfortunately, we couldn't reach the final, but we had a great run that season with Mourinho. Both he and Carlo are great coaches but different. When you speak of players you say there are strikers,

JE NE REGRETTE RIEN, 2011–13

there are midfielders, there are defenders and there are great ones in all positions, but they are different in some respects.

It's like this with Mourinho and Ancelotti, they are both great coaches but maybe they have a different approach, but the winning mentality was the same, you know, they're two of the best coaches ever, Mourinho and Carlo. Carlo brought us calmness and experience and we played really great under him those first two years when he arrived and we won La Décima – that was like the best feeling. Everyone was talking about it and everyone was desperate to win it, so it was a great feeling when we managed to win it.

In the locker room, when it was announced that Carlo was coming to be the coach, everyone was really excited to see that Carlo was coming because we knew everything about him and the teams that he coached, the titles, the Champions Leagues that he had won, and the teams that he coached, and everyone was excited about having such a great and experienced coach because we wanted to reach the next level with him and because we had a great team, and he was like the icing on the cake. I have big trust and big confidence from Carlo. From the beginning he was clear with what he wanted from me and how important I am for the team. That helped me a lot to show my quality on the pitch.

He was really everything that I expected from such a coach who had won so much with other teams. He coached one of the best Milan teams in history; he coached great teams like Paris, like Chelsea, like Bayern, like others, and everything that he brought, you expected from him – quality, man-management, experience – everything. You could see that he was also a great player, and he transmitted that positive energy towards us, and we played a great season, and we won the cup against Barcelona and then the Champions League against Atlético.

The way we won it was amazing. If you look at that goal that we scored so deep into extra time and watched Carlo to see his celebration, it looks like this goal, which comes so late in the game, was not at the last second to equalise and go to extra time but maybe just at the very start of the game. He was so calm, and this is what he always transmitted to us. Knowing that you have someone who believes in you, who gives you freedom to express yourself – it was really nice to play in that first period under him.

When he returned it was as if he had never been away. He was the same. More experienced, obviously. He had been at some great clubs, and he had done great jobs but he didn't change for me at all. He was the same Carlo – calmness, all the things that I told you before and he had all this again, he brought all this to the team again.

I don't know how Carlo managed to be so calm. It's unbelievable. I think that all this apart, he's a great coach and he knows football amazingly well. He understands football but all these results that he managed to do is, I think, because of his personality – the way he acts, the way he behaves, the respect he has for everybody, no matter what is their job in the club – that's why he is so successful for me.

Carlo sees that his job is to instil confidence and I think that he does this perfectly. Whenever you have some tough defeats, like we all have, he transmits positive energy and confidence into players. He always says, 'No matter what, I still think you are the best players – you are the best team and so you will show this. Stay calm. Keep confidence and keep doing what you're doing and we will find a way to go through a difficult period and just believe in yourself. I believe in you. You are all great players, great people, and that's why we will find a way out of everything, of this situation.'

This is really him, this is what he gives his players, and when you have someone like this it's easier, because in football there are many ups and downs, because in these days you easily get criticised, there are so many opinions and everything and if you listen to a voice outside then a player can easily lose confidence, but when you have someone like Carlo it's easier to manage all this, especially as a group.

He genuinely loves his players. You know that he sides with the players and that you can completely trust him, that you can talk with him not just about football. Maybe if you have some issue outside of football, you can speak with him easily, without a problem, he will listen, he will try to help. I remember when he arrived here in Madrid and we went for pre-season, first in the United States, and when we came back, he asked me if I was

THE DREAM

alone in Madrid, and I was alone because my family was in Croatia and he was also alone. I said yes and he called me for a dinner, and we went for a dinner where we live and I was a bit, not shocked but, surprised, so happy. Can you imagine the coach calling you, 'Let's have a dinner, let's talk about anything.' And this is Carlo, and then when you know you have a coach like this you want to give even more for him on the pitch and this is like something that left me really like, wow, not just a coach, what a guy, what a person. When you look at titles, he is there, but now we can always discuss this and that, and in terms of human beings he is top, he is top, for sure.

It's not easy to be coach here many years, it takes a lot away from you because of the pressure. You don't have any room for mistakes, or to not win every year, and he is managing and winning all the time, that's why he is still here and it's not easy. The pressure is huge, you just have to win. This is only what works here – to win. You have to be all the time at the top of your game, you cannot relax, not even for one second. Even friendly games, for example, we need to win. It happened a few times where you win the Champions League and then in the start of pre-season you lose one or two games and the questions start – 'Why this? This is not good! What's happening?' – you know, it's crazy. You know, at my other clubs I never had this level of expectation. Here winning is an obligation. Everyone wants to win but nowhere are you pushed as much as you are here. That's why Madrid, for me, is the best and biggest club ever.

PART FOUR

MADRID

13

THE FIFTH TIME, 2013–14

The relationship between the Champions League and Real Madrid is so special because it is born out of Madrid's extraordinary history in the competition.

On 13 June 1956 the very first final of the European Cup was played in the Parc des Princes in Paris. Everyone knows who won the inaugural competition, but not many people can remember who Real Madrid played against. It was a French club: Reims. And Reims were 2–0 up after ten minutes. Then the great Alfredo Di Stéfano, the only player on the pitch who was neither Spanish nor French, scored Real's first ever goal in a European Cup final. It was 2–2 after half an hour. Michel Hidalgo, who would go on to coach France to the European Championship in 1984, put Reims ahead again halfway through the second half. Real got their winner in the 79th minute. And a legend was born.

The European Cup was won for the first five years by Real Madrid. The royal club of world football gave the competition glamour. Those five consecutive wins established the idea that if any team was going to conquer Europe, it had to be good enough to beat Real. Seven decades on from the creation of the European Cup, that still feels true today.

And now that club was asking for me. For the second time. The first time I would have been interested in going and even signed a preliminary contract. But the key clause I insisted on was that I would come only with the blessing of my current employers. Milan wanted me to stay, which I did.

In the summer of 2013 I was still contracted to PSG but felt no such loyalty. Despite their behaviour earlier in the season, they were oddly reluctant to let me leave a year early. But I eventually managed to extract myself. I made my dissatisfaction clear and they probably realised that a dissatisfied manager would not be likely to deliver the success they demanded. It was best for both parties to go our separate ways.

At the Bernabéu, the unveiling of a new coach or a new signing is done with a great sense of theatre. Before I was presented to the Madridistas, there was a private moment that neither public nor press was privy to. I was taken into the trophy room by the president, Florentino Pérez. There was no sign of any of the cups the club had won domestically. Instead, he walked me past the row of European Cups that the club had won throughout its glorious history. The years were all there: 1956, 1957, 1958, 1959, 1960, 1966, 1998, 2000, 2002. Nine in all. But there was a gap there for a tenth

THE FIFTH TIME, 2013–14

trophy. The president just looked at me and said, 'Beautiful, very beautiful, but there's one missing.'

This had become the obsession of the club and of its fans. La Décima, they called it. A mythical tenth trophy. They had a shortish wait between the fifth and sixth, then a very long wait between the sixth and the seventh. Thirty-two years. Then there was another gold rush. Three wins in five years. The ninth win starred Zidane and Figo, two of the greatest *galácticos* in the club's history. Since then, other foreign stars had come – Ronaldo, Beckham, Owen, van Nistelrooy, Higuaín, Robben, Sneijder, Kaká, Özil. And these are just the attacking players – I'm not even listing the defenders they also bought. They are all of them great talents, but none of them provided the solution to the drought. Nor all the many coaches who were bussed in season after season and given too little time to achieve results. In 2009 Pérez was re-installed as club president on the promise that he would finally bring the waiting to an end.

By the time I got a call from Madrid, the wait for La Décima had been going on for 11 years. It had cost a lot of money to bring in all those coaches and then pay them compensation after they got the sack. While they waited, Real had to watch Barcelona win the Champions League three times, Milan twice, plus three different English clubs. For six seasons in a row, they were eliminated in the round of 16. It was in the middle of this run, in 2006, that they first sounded me out about coming to Madrid. After Real's sixth consecutive elimination before the quarter-finals, their solution was to hire the coach who'd won it twice with two different clubs: Porto in 2004, Inter in 2010 – José Mourinho.

He arrived in Real on the back of that second win. For the next three seasons he made a lot of progress, especially with the mentality of the team. He ended Barcelona's period of dominance in La Liga. In one season he broke the record for the most points, goals and wins. And he greatly improved on the club's recent performances in the Champions League, reaching the semi-final for three years in a row. But as ever he brought drama with him. In his second season he even managed to get banned to the stands for two matches in the Champions League. He did not get on with two of the club's most culturally important players: the keeper and captain, Iker Casillas, and the indomitable Sergio Ramos, the beating hearts of the club. Both had won the World Cup and the Euros representing Spain. But Mourinho dropped Casillas, and he didn't see eye to eye with Ramos.

So for the second time in my career, I inherited a squad that had been coached by Mourinho. At Chelsea two other coaches had come in between, but the players were mainly his. Now at Real I was hired to win the Champions League and keep an entire squad of superstars happy. Pérez even referred to me as 'a peacemaker'.

There were already a lot of big names to manage. As well as Casillas and Ramos, there was Cristiano Ronaldo and Karim Benzema, Xabi Alonso and Luka Modrić, Sami Khedira and

THE FIFTH TIME, 2013–14

Ángel Di María. The summer I moved to Madrid, they also bought three players who were still only 21: Dani Carvajal, Casemiro and Isco. Then they broke two transfer records. Asier Illarramendi became the most expensive Spanish player that Real had ever bought. And then they went and paid more than had ever been spent on any footballer, ever, anywhere, acquiring Gareth Bale for €100 million from Spurs.

I had worked with some very big stars in my time, and had somehow found a way to turn them into a team and keep them all more or less on my side. But I'd never had quite so many lavish talents to choose from. But then, I'd never managed Real Madrid before.

The influx of younger players, either bought in or promoted from the academy, brought other challenges. At a club like Madrid these youngsters have many more responsibilities than they used to. These mainly come from outside, because of the sheer weight of media attention. It's the manager's responsibility not to add to that pressure. But as I get older, the players always stay young, so the generational gap between us is always growing. It has been an unexpected part of my job to adapt to social and cultural changes, and work out the best way to manage such changes. I can't demand that the players adapt to me. Each country, each club, each language and each culture bring extra layers of change, and as the game globalises so the complexity increases.

Meanwhile, managing the young players at Madrid is not like at smaller clubs. We do not have time to let a young man mature as a person and a player in the first team. We cannot give them minutes for their own sake. They can only play if they are good enough, if they are ready. Our job is to win games. Our job, ultimately and always, is to win the Champions League.

Obviously, I wasn't completely uninvolved in the new acquisitions. Just as I arrived, the club said that they were trying to buy Bale. 'Carlo,' they said, 'what do you think about him? Tell us whether you believe he can be a Real Madrid player.' Even when you are buying the very best players in the world, at a club like Real Madrid you are obliged to ask these kinds of questions – yes, this boy is good, we know he can play but can he do it at one of the most famous clubs in the world? My response was unequivocal. I knew he could do it at Madrid, and he did. He looked at home from his first touch of the ball in his first training session. He was straight in the team, and he had a great first season. Modrić helped him to settle in because they were friends from their days at Spurs.

Isco had shone in the European Under-21 Championship that summer in which Spain had triumphed. He looked to me like a grafter who would transform the team's work ethic on the pitch. And I was used to owners going out and splashing cash on players and expecting me to pick them. At Milan I had Ronaldinho and Ronaldo sprung on me. At Chelsea there was the Torres saga. That was my job, to take all the big, big players and turn them into a cohesive unit.

THE FIFTH TIME, 2013–14

To get Bale and Cristiano Ronaldo to play together up front, to help Di María and Modrić get their form back, to find a solution to the problem of Casillas.

On top of these, I also had to get my head down and learn a fourth language. I found learning Spanish easier than Bale did, so it was very helpful to have the English speaker Paul Clement join me and help with Bale's integration into the squad.

My other great advantage was to be joined on the bench by Zinedine Zidane. Since retiring in 2006, he had been the de facto head coach of Real Madrid's B team. I say 'de facto' because technically Santiago Sánchez was the head coach and Zidane, who did not have the necessary coaching badges, was his assistant. He did that job for two seasons and then became my assistant. It was of course useful to me that he had a very good relationship with Pérez. Of more immediate help was his knowledge of the young players who had joined the squad from the B team and the academy.

When I was presented to the world by the president, he said very complimentary things. 'His style and character fit the profile of this club perfectly. He is a proper football man, an intelligent man and a natural winner. He is the coach our directors and members wanted the most and he was also the coach I wanted the most.' So, all in all, I felt very positive as I took up my new role. But I knew from the start that I was at Madrid for one reason and one reason only. There was that empty space on the shelf in the trophy room, and it was my job to fill it. If I too could not win La Décima, I would be out. I understood this and I got to work.

Despite the noise around Mourinho, he had assembled a team that I found in rude health. He had done a fantastic job changing the mentality of the squad and ending the supremacy of their great rivals Barcelona. The fans appreciated him and still do. But he had left me with a problem in the shape of Casillas. Mourinho had dropped him in favour of Diego López and now I had to work out how to resolve the situation. Should I restore him to the role of first-choice goalkeeper and to the captaincy? I had experienced selection problems before, when I arrived at Milan when there were more forwards than I could fit into any system. But at least with outfield players you could keep them happy by bringing them off the bench during a game. They at least got some game time. With a keeper, you must pick one or the other, and that can create resentment in the one not being picked.

I thought about it and, while I don't like sitting on the fence, I concluded that the best answer was a compromise. They were both good keepers and there wasn't a huge difference between them. My plan was to play a defensive high line, and I thought López with his superior speed was better suited to the role. But he didn't have the experience in the Champions League that Casillas had. In 1999 Casillas became the youngest keeper ever to play in the competition, and at 19 in 2000 he was the youngest keeper to play in the final and win it. In the 2002 final he was on the bench but came off it when the first choice got injured and made several important saves to help keep out Bayer Leverkusen. Casillas was the only survivor of that squad who was still waiting for another Champions League win 11 years later. But he was a Madridista and had the competition running through his veins.

So I decided to rotate. I would play López in La Liga and Casillas in the knockout competitions – the Copa del Rey and the Champions League. I spoke to them both before I made my choice public. Neither was particularly happy to know that for at least some of the season they would be on the bench. The positive outcome was that both were highly motivated. And I think it took some of the pressure off López to know that he wasn't keeping a Madrid legend out of the side week in, week out. By the end of that first season, López had played 37 games and Casillas 24. The last of them was to be the club's most important game in 12 years.

As usual I went into the group games that autumn with the same ambition as ever: to get through the group unscathed and, if possible, qualify before all the games had been played, then rest some players for the last fixtures. Low-maintenance progress is the ideal, with no injuries and not too much fatigue.

But at the same time, I had to work out how to fit together all the moving parts of my squad. Mourinho had been hired to win at all costs and his style of football wasn't necessarily one that Madridistas were used to. Club tradition had appeared to take a back seat. He seemed comfortable with football that brought few goals and so his system prioritised not conceding. He was happy for scoring to be a form of counterpunch. The formation that the team had got used to playing under Mourinho was a 4–3–3. I hadn't used it much before, so at first I thought of reverting to my old preference for 4–4–2, playing Ronaldo alongside Benzema as a twin strike force. But from talking to Ronaldo it soon became clear that he preferred to play in a wide position and attack from there. If that's what he preferred, I wasn't about to ask him to switch. In his three seasons with Mourinho he had scored 53 goals, then 60, then 55. An astonishing record. So we went with a set-up that had Ronaldo cutting in onto his right foot from the left. It worked. In my first season he got 51, then 61 in my second. In the Champions League group stage alone he got nine: a record for any player in the competition.

Then on the right I could choose either Bale or Di María, who were both left-footed. The advantage of having such pacy and skilful players in those flank positions is the possibility for counter-attacking. It would be hard for defenders to contain them. Bale started on the bench in that first Champions League game but came on for a 30-minute cameo to get the feel of playing for Madrid at this highest of levels.

THE FIFTH TIME, 2013–14

In the hole behind Benzema I began with Isco to play in a role similar to the one taken by Kaká at Milan. Holding the centre behind him were Khedira and Modrić. But the more games I oversaw, the more I felt able to change things. The second game I went more with a four-strong midfield. By the third game I was refining the system into something like a 4–2–1–3, with Benzema at the centre of the front three, Bale and Ronaldo as the wide players and Modrić as the 10 in the hole.

By the fourth game, our toughest of the group, away to Juventus, we were close to our strongest team in the most balanced shape yet. Bale started on the right, Ronaldo on the left. Ramos, who was more used to playing in central defence, sat behind Bale at right back, with Khedira able to come across from the right of the midfield to add cover. That shored up that flank when we were out of possession. Marcelo and Modrić performed the same function on the left side of the pitch. I also had Xabi Alonso back after a long absence through injury. He sat at the base of midfield and controlled our rhythm. With Ramos on the right, I put Pepe and Rafaël Varane in central defence.

It went like clockwork. In the group phase we scored 20 goals and finished on 16 points, which is the highest tally any team of mine had ever achieved. Galatasaray were beaten 10–2 on aggregate, Copenhagen 6–0 on aggregate. It was only away to Juventus that we dropped points in a 2–2 draw.

THE DREAM

In the fifth match I was free to give a game to younger players like Casemiro and Illarramendi.

Topping the group meant we avoided being drawn against any of the sides I'd rather not face, including two of my former clubs: Chelsea and PSG. There was also a chance of drawing Milan, but luckily, they were avoided. Instead, we got Schalke 04. I mean no disrespect to any club, but naturally some opponents hold less fear than others, and all any coach wants is to move through each round.

In the knockout stages each tie, indeed each game, has to be approached differently with each opponent investigated fully and specific plans and players selected to win that particular game. So it was with Schalke. For the away leg in Gelsenkirchen, I went for a 4–3–3 with Alonso holding the centre, flanked by Modrić and Di María, who were there to prepare the ammunition for a strike force that the media soon dubbed the BBC: Benzema, Bale, Cristiano. It turned out to be a BBC show. They all scored two, in that order. Bale's driving run and a little pass from Ronaldo set up Benzema for the first. Then Benzema won possession on the right and passed to Bale, who scored a wonderful individual goal with an intricate dribble. Bale's long pass fed Ronaldo to dink past his marker for the third. Ronaldo's back flick put Benzema through for the fourth. Ramos feinted a clever through-ball for Bale to drive home the fifth. Then Benzema fed Ronaldo who rounded the keeper for the sixth. They all brought something different, and on that form, they made

THE FIFTH TIME, 2013–14

us look unbeatable. In fact, the best goal of the night was left until last when Klaas-Jan Huntelaar volleyed in from the edge of the box in injury time for Schalke.

I did my very best in the pre-match talk to insist that the second leg was not a dead rubber, that this was still a serious game. It seemed to fall on deaf ears because it was a stale first half that brought a goal apiece. I asked for more urgency in the second half and got two goals in two minutes. A 9–2 aggregate win brought us to the next round and more German opposition. But this was going to be no pushover.

At the time German football had a lot of strength in depth. The previous season's final was between two of its clubs, Bayern Munich and Borussia Dortmund. Bayern Munich were the winners. They won narrowly, with a goal scored in the very last minute. Dortmund won their semi-final against Real, outpowering them to win 4–3 on aggregate. And that's who we now had to beat. Their very good side had a spine of Mats Hummels, Marco Reus and Robert Lewandowski, although he was thankfully suspended for the first leg. But the real secret weapon and tactical mastermind was their coach, Jürgen Klopp. I was to have many encounters with him over the next decade.

At the Bernabéu I went with the same 4–3–3 formation that proved so destructive against Schalke. With Di María ill, I put Isco on the left and the system carried on working. We dominated from the start. Bale took a cutback from Carvajal, who was playing at right back, and muscled his way

THE DREAM

through to finish. Isco scored a second from the edge of the box. Ronaldo and Bale, taking free kicks from distance, both drew almost identical saves from Dortmund's flying keeper Roman Weidenfeller. On the hour Modrić coolly intercepted a clearance and fed Ronaldo for our third.

In the media it was assumed that the tie was now a done deal. But they hadn't factored in that Lewandowski would be back, and we all knew that he had scored four at home in the previous season's semi-final against Real. So I repeated my team talk. If you can win 3–0 at home, you can lose 3–0 away, especially at a place like Dortmund. It has a tightly enclosed stadium and not to mention the Yellow Wall. The venue and the fans make for a very intimidating atmosphere when things are not going your way. My insistence that the tie was not over seemed to be contradicted by my decision to rest Ronaldo, who had a niggling knee injury. It was as if I was saying we didn't need his goals. His calm would certainly have helped when we got an early penalty, which Di María took. Weidenfeller brilliantly saved it and then Dortmund had nothing to lose. They flew at us, while we seemed to go into our shells.

In the first half it was a sign of our nervousness that Pepe thought he was heading the ball back to Casillas. Instead, he nodded it to Reus, who didn't have much to do to make it 1–0. Reus scored again when he pounced on another loose ball, played in Lewandowski and crashed in his rebounded shot. Our lead in the tie was down to one, and there were still 45 minutes to go. I looked around the dressing room at

THE FIFTH TIME, 2013–14

half-time and thought we seemed down, afraid even. I tried making a change, injecting some of Isco's energy on the right, but it didn't help much. In the second half the traffic went only one way. Luckily, at least, we had Casillas, who made two brilliant saves at crucial moments.

The history of knockout football in the Champions League repeats the same lesson over and over. Beware of complacency. Never assume a game is over. Don't give the opposition any encouragement. We all know the lesson in theory. In practice it's sometimes hard to follow. So it proved against Dortmund. Real won 3–2, but we survived by the skin of our teeth, thanks to all the defensive discipline we'd practised on the training pitch with Pepe and Ramos flanked by Fábio Coentrão and Carvajal. Above all, there was Casillas. He more than justified my decision to give him the gloves and the captaincy in this competition, one that he knew so well.

It was shaping up to be a positive first season. We were going well in La Liga, chasing Atlético Madrid for the title. We had beaten them in the semi-final of the Copa del Rey to set up a final against Barcelona. But first and foremost we had to take on yet another German opponent. Bayern were the holders, although this season they were under the management of Pep Guardiola. If we managed to beat them, too, Real Madrid could probably have claimed the unofficial title of German champions.

History was on our side. Since the European Cup became the Champions League, the holders had not yet

THE DREAM

successfully retained the trophy. Only three winners had ever made it back to the final. It was hard to clamber to the summit two years running. All the same, I had every reason to be worried. As coach of Barcelona, Guardiola had a good record at the Bernabéu and he was enjoying an excellent first season at Bayern. They were way ahead in the Bundesliga and there was quality all the way through the team, from Manuel Neuer in goal to Jérôme Boateng in defence, Bastian Schweinsteiger and Philipp Lahm in midfield, and Franck Ribéry and Arjen Robben on either flank. They also had two players – Robert Alaba and Toni Kroos – who would one day find their way to Madrid. We knew that both legs would be very difficult, but we felt that our team for the first leg was well balanced with Alonso able to double up by holding the centre and also protecting the back line. This enabled Modrić and Di María to support and supply the front three.

Before the home leg came the final of the Copa del Rey in Valencia. The score against Barcelona was 1–1 with five minutes to go when we drove out of defence on the left and Bale picked up the ball on the wing, pushed it past the last defender and sprinted like Usain Bolt, famously leaving the pitch to get past him and bear down on the box, where he poked the ball past their keeper. His winner was a wonder goal, worthy of someone for whom Madrid had broken that world transfer record. His team-mates were ecstatic. So were the fans. Even I had to smile. But Bale then caught the

THE FIFTH TIME, 2013–14

flu and I was forced to make changes to the team that had dismantled Dortmund at home. In what was essentially a 4–1–2–3, I pushed Isco forward into the role taken by Bale.

It was a contest between two teams with different philosophies. Our players needed space to move the ball very quickly. Guardiola wanted to control possession in order to create space. It's important to be aware of this when setting up a team. Do not worry about limited possession. You have to focus on defending well, and at the moment you gain possession show your quality offensively.

The match statistics reflect that. We had 36 per cent possession and completed 270 passes to their 700. We also collectively ran 6 kilometres less than them. But the metric that really matters was in our favour. There was only one goal in the game, which we scored on the counter-attack in the first half. Coentrão surged down the left and crossed for Benzema to side-foot into an empty net.

Naturally I worried about going to Munich and protecting such a narrow lead after the stage fright we had suffered in Dortmund. But I shouldn't have. The players were motivated by the target of reaching the final after 12 years. They had fallen at this last hurdle for the previous three years. We played the perfect game. Again, Bayern had much more possession and so completed many more passes. But their need to overcome our lead opened up the field of play. We sat deep in two banks of four, in what nowadays is known as a low block. Whenever a move of theirs broke down we counter-attacked at pace. And when the chances came our way, we took almost all of them. In a five-minute period, two headers from an unmarked Ramos put us two up after 20 minutes. One was from a Modrić corner, the other from a Di María free kick. In another 15 minutes Bale put in Ronaldo to make it three. In the second half Guardiola strangely replaced his only striker with a midfielder, which hardly increased the threat we faced. The contest was already over when Ronaldo added a fourth from a free kick in the final minute.

So in two rounds we had eliminated both finalists from the previous season. Now all we had to do to win La Décima was beat this year's finalist also. And we knew them well. They were Atlético Madrid.

The city was plunged into a collective fever for the next month as the countdown began. Obviously, it was difficult to avoid getting sucked into it. I was privately relieved to duck the more personal drama of playing Chelsea in the final. It would have meant planning to beat John Terry and Ashley Cole, in a team that once again was managed by Mourinho. It was his fourth semi-final defeat in four seasons since he'd last won it.

Instead, my opposite number in the Estádio da Luz in Lisbon would be the Argentine coach, Diego Simeone. He was a very popular figure among the Atlético half of the city. In his playing days he had spent two separate spells at the club. Until he became coach at the end of 2011, Atlético had

THE FIFTH TIME, 2013–14

employed the same revolving-door policy as Real. They'd had five coaches in three years. But they stayed loyal to Simeone, and he began winning hearts and minds and cups. The latest of them was their first La Liga title since 1996, which they won a week before the Champions League final. We dropped seven points in our last three games and finished third. Pérez was not happy with this, so before the final there was talk in the media about whether I'd survive the summer. The pursuit of La Décima became an even bigger game for me. Everything rested on it.

I tried to project calm. I noticed that Paul Clement was looking a bit apprehensive ahead of the game and I asked him if it was his first final in the competition. He admitted it was.

'It's my seventh,' I said.

It was a historic occasion for two reasons. Atlético had not been this far in the competition in 40 years. And it was the first ever final between two teams from the same city. It was all set to be a clash of styles. Simeone sent out sides to win at all costs, to play a brutalist type of football. The key elements of his style were passion, aggression, discipline and team spirit. His talisman up front was Diego Costa, a burly old-school centre-forward who took no prisoners. In fact, he was a big doubt before the game and only lasted eight minutes before he had to leave the pitch early.

My selection ahead of the match was mainly focused on trying to fill a hole left by Xabi Alonso, who was suspended.

This was damaging for us because he was one of the best in the world at providing a stable base in midfield. Of the options to replace him I could have selected Casemiro, but it seemed too early in his career for such a responsibility. The main alternatives were Illarramendi or Khedira, whose match fitness was in doubt after recently returning from several months out with a torn anterior cruciate ligament. He'd had only two games and even he thought he was a risk at only two-thirds fitness.

'I need that 60/70 per cent on the pitch for maybe 60/70 per cent of the time,' I told him. Ronaldo said something similar to him: 'I don't care if you are 70 per cent – we need you on the pitch.' To hear it from such a team-mate was probably more inspirational to him than anything I could say. In the event, it worked. He lasted an hour and played well.

Of my other worries, Pepe came to me and said, 'I cannot play.' He's a warrior and if he says he cannot play, then he cannot play. Varane came in to replace him, though I kept Pepe on the bench just in case. Then there were my three front players. The BBC. All had doubts over them, most of all Benzema, who in the end lasted 80 minutes.

Atlético played as I expected. They were well organised, harriers when chasing the ball, and they did their very best to make sure that Ronaldo's freedom of expression was restricted. With ten minutes or so to go in the first half, Atlético won a corner. There was a messy game of aerial pinball

THE FIFTH TIME, 2013-14

as we failed to clear. Casillas came out to stop the mayhem but only ended in no-man's land and the Atlético stopper Diego Godín managed to loop a header over him. It was far from the most beautiful goal ever scored in the final, but it looked like being one of the most significant. Our three best chances in the match fell to Bale, one before their goal, two after. For whatever reason he was unable to take them.

We suffered a lot. There was no space to play. But we kept trying and trying. We had nearly two-thirds of the possession and completed twice as many passes as Atlético. We were being beaten at our own counter-attacking game. The clock ticked down so far that UEFA officials were tying red and white ribbons on the arms of the trophy. The 90 minutes were up. We were three minutes into injury time when we won a corner on the right. Modrić curled it in and somewhere in the melee Ramos rose to meet it. He headed the ball firmly into the bottom left corner. Thibault Courtois didn't move.

It was a genuinely dramatic equaliser. No wonder Casillas, who was at fault for their goal, kissed his team-mate's forehead at the final whistle. You can call us lucky, but we had worked for it and we deserved it. It seemed to puncture Atlético, who had worked so hard and didn't have much left to give in attack. But their ability to resist meant that the game could easily go to penalties, and that seemed probable for the first 20 minutes of extra time. Then Di María went on a brilliant run down the left, tricking three tired defenders

THE DREAM

as he cut into the box and shot. Courtois stretched out a leg and the ball looped up towards the far post, where Bale was arriving to nod it in. In an instant, all our misses were forgotten. Two minutes later Marcelo, on as a sub, attacked down the same channel as Di María to give us a third, and at the very end Ronaldo was fouled and scored from the spot.

The Atlético fans were incredible and carried on cheering as the game ran away from them. As for Real's fans, they could finally breathe a sigh of relief. So could the president. I had my own moment of personal reward during the press conference after the game. I was talking when a group of players invaded the room, jumped on me and began singing 'How could I not love you?'

Very late that night we were tired and very emotional as we got back to Madrid and witnessed a reception like nothing I had ever known. Seeing so many people on the streets celebrating the trophy was something I will not forget for the rest of my life. The club had the precious La Décima at last and I had my fifth.

14

DER WANDERER, 2014–19

In the summer of 2014, the World Cup was hosted by Brazil and won by Germany. As with every such competition, the top clubs go shopping, and Real were no different.

We bought the winner of the Golden Boot, James Rodríguez. He had already caught the eye playing for Monaco, where he got the most assists of any player in Ligue 1 history. But now he had scored six goals on the world stage and won the Golden Boot even though Colombia made it no further than the quarter-final. Naturally the press wondered how on earth I was going to fit him into a side that already contained BBC. But Madrid's history shows that they always want to have the best players – especially ones who are signed not just for the present but for the future too.

The other big signing arrived in possession of a World Cup winner's medal. Toni Kroos was part of the Germany side that demolished Brazil 7–1 in the semi. He scored two goals in three minutes. Then they beat Argentina in a tight

THE DREAM

final. He had already won three Bundesligas and the Champions League with Bayern, so was clearly not going to be intimidated by the challenge of pulling on the white shirt.

Some of our own players arrived back for the new season wanting to forget the summer. Spain were the holders but managed to lose 5–1 in their opening game to the Netherlands, who they had beaten in the previous final. Then Chile beat them, and they were eliminated after 180 minutes. (It was just as bad for Italy and England, who were drawn in the same group and finished third and fourth.)

With such a crowded squad, it was going to take a lot of work to keep everyone happy. Di María, who had a good World Cup, asked for a transfer. I didn't want him to leave. He was a penetrative player who had an incredible record setting up goals for others. His assists were second only to Messi during his time in Spain. But the club didn't offer him a contract that made him feel valued. This is one of the side effects of joining Real Madrid, especially for attacking players. There is always an incoming tide of fresh talent challenging for places. I also lost Xabi Alonso. Of course, Xabi has now joined the list of players I have coached who went on to have good careers as coaches themselves – Zidane, Seedorf, Inzaghi, Lampard, Deschamps, Conte, Rijkaard and Gullit among them. And now Xabi has the task of taking Madrid back to the Champions League summit.

We missed him and Di María at the start of the season, which did not go well. But then we began our defence of the Champions League and beat Basel 5–1. After that, we could not stop scoring goals in La Liga: 8–2, 5–1, 5–0, 5–0. We went to Anfield and beat Liverpool 3–0, then beat them 1–0 at home. We also won El Clásico 3–1. It was the first time Real had beaten Barcelona by more than a single goal in six seasons. 'MORE THAN A VICTORY,' said one of the sporting papers on their front page.

The squad was developing into something special, something with its own identity. They were enjoying the process of renewal and adaptation that is a necessary part of football.

And so it went on. Kroos was fitting in. So was Rodríguez, first on the left, then on the right of a 4–4–2. As we accumulated win after win after win, Florentino Pérez announced that the club would be happy to renew my contract at the end of the season. 'He creates a great family atmosphere apart from doing a great job as coach,' said the president. 'This is important.' It's always nice to have support from the top, but I knew that nice lasts only as long as the good results last.

Real ended the year in Morocco, where that season's Club World Cup was held. We beat the Argentine club San Lorenzo in the final. It brought our tally of consecutive wins to 22. I had been coaching for the best part of 20 years and had experienced nothing like this.

So what went wrong? In the first game of 2015 our run came to an end when we lost to Valencia. The spell wasn't immediately broken. But around that time UEFA issued statistics that showed that Real trained less than other top

THE DREAM

clubs. Senior people at the club insisted that the squad must try harder on the training ground. I was of the opposite view. We were suffering from tiredness and injuries, and these came from overwork. At a crucial moment I had to do without Ramos, Rodríguez, Pepe, Benzema and, perhaps most importantly and for four months, Modrić. There were no like-for-like replacements for the last two, who were special players in our system. In this period, we also lost to Atlético and Barcelona, our nearest rivals in La Liga.

There was another problem, which was to do with Bale. The president got annoyed when I substituted him in the game where we lost our winning streak, and he took it personally. In the next game Bale was booed for not passing to Ronaldo when there was an open goal. A fan expressed frustration by targeting Bale's car. This was a headache I could have done without, and I started to feel as if the club, which had so recently talked of renewing my contract, were losing faith in me. If I had created a family I had to accept that families often fight, but they should always remain family.

Admittedly, in the second season there were problems with Bale. He wanted to play in a central position and his agent went so far as to go behind my back to the president to try and make this happen. Naturally, this was not good for my relationship with the player. I received a call that the president wanted to speak with me at the end of training that day. This was very unusual. He told me about Bale's agent coming to his office. I explained that, yes, Bale certainly had world-class qualities, but I was trying to help him understand his core strengths so he could fulfil his potential. I was pretty sure I was better qualified than Bale's agent or my president to help him with that. Later I told Bale to come directly to me next time. He simply said, 'Yes, OK, no problem.'

As ever the Champions League was a place where we hoped to silence all critics. In our group we accumulated maximum points. Six games, six wins. In the first knockout stage in February, at a time when there were doubts about us domestically, we went to Gelsenkirchen and beat Schalke 2–0. In the return leg Casillas made two quite bad errors and gifted them two goals. Headers from Ronaldo kept us level. It went to 3–3 and on 84 minutes they made it 4–3. Casillas made a save that kept us in the tie, but the truth is we easily could have been eliminated. Fans were showing their displeasure as only Madridistas can, and I didn't blame them. In attack and defence we lacked fight, motivation and concentration. It was not good for our image or that of the club. The whistles were justified.

It wasn't a positive launchpad for the quarter-final, which pitted us against Atlético. The portent for the tie was not great either. That season we had played our local rivals six times and not managed to beat them once. By the end of the first leg away, that run had extended to seven. It was a typically tense game where no one wanted to give anything away. Bale, playing on the right of a 4–4–2, had the best chance very early on. We had more of the possession but could not

THE DREAM

break them down. It was almost a repeat of Lisbon. It was the same for almost all of the second leg. When they had a man sent off with a quarter of an hour to go, the odds tilted in our favour. The player dismissed happened to be Ronaldo's marker. Sure enough, in the 88th minute Ronaldo set off on a blistering run down the right, executed a neat one-two with Rodríguez and slid the ball across the box, where the player waiting to tap in was Javier Hernández. He was the first Mexican to play for Real since Hugo Sánchez. We had taken him on loan from Manchester United and he was deputising for Benzema.

The win didn't manage to quieten any of the noise because the domestic season was coming to the boil and our semi-final opponents were Juventus. Again, injuries forced my hand and as we travelled to Turin I picked Ramos to fill the hole left by the injured Modrić. Bale joined Ronaldo up front. The return to one of my old clubs brought a reunion with Pirlo, who was playing out his career in Italy at Juve. And then there was Álvaro Morata, who had joined Real as a boy of 16. He asked for more game time and so we had let him go in the summer with a clause in the contract that allowed us to buy him back. He tapped in after Casillas pushed a Carlos Tevez shot into his path, but understandably he didn't feel like celebrating. Ronaldo equalised from close range. Then Rodríguez's diving header came back off the crossbar. If it had gone in, we'd have had the two away goals that could have taken us to the final. Instead they went down the other end, where Tevez was brought down and scored from the resulting penalty.

In the Champions League, if you have courage you win. If you have fear, you lose. The continued absence of Modrić and Benzema did seem to instil a slight concern in me. Maybe the players felt that emotion. With defensive players moved into the midfield the balance of the side was altered and it put too much pressure on Rodríguez to be the answer to all our attacking prayers.

In the second leg back at home we did everything we could to bring the game back in our favour. We dominated in the first half and went ahead when Rodríguez was brought down in the box and Ronaldo scored from the spot. We were leading in the tie but two of my own former players now conspired against Real. Pirlo's free kick from the right was punched away by Casillas, headed back in, and nodded on by Paul Pogba into the path of Morata. As he waited for the bouncing ball to come under control, he must have had time to think about what would happen next. But again, he made no mistake. And again, he didn't celebrate.

There was more than half an hour to go but we simply couldn't get the goal that would equalise the tie. Juventus were back in the final for the first time since my Milan side beat them in 2003. We didn't win La Liga either, despite winning nine of our last ten games, and scoring a record 118 goals. But that earlier stutter in the season, and a draw with Valencia in early May, cost us. We finished second by two points to a rampant Barcelona. That month Zinedine Zidane, who had been coaching the reserves, got his UEFA pro coaching licence.

Would I stay or would I go? That was a question for the president. But the omens did not look good. The last time a Real coach had survived a season without winning anything was more than 30 years earlier. The man they didn't sack was Alfredo Di Stéfano, the greatest player in the club's history. Sure enough, Pérez announced that the club had decided to move on.

'It was a very difficult decision to make,' he told the press, adding that 'here the demands are very high, and we need to give Real Madrid a new push that allows us to reach the level that we want to be. The affection that the players and the fans have for Carlo is the same as the affection I myself have for him.'

I knew this might come, and that talk of a contract renewal was meaningless without results. The good-looking statistics were not enough to save me either – more than 300 goals and winning three-quarters of our games. All you can do in football is shrug and move on. And yet there was something curious about the press conference where my removal was announced. 'What did Ancelotti do wrong?' said Pérez. 'I don't know,' he answered his own question.

I was able to leave Madrid with my head held high, having delivered La Décima that the club craved. Just as when I left Chelsea, the players were generous. Rafael Benítez took the

DER WANDERER, 2014–19

job but Pérez lost patience halfway through the season and replaced him with Zidane. Zidane had been a Banquo in waiting. He was one of the few Madrid players who could rival Di Stéfano for legendary status. The side we had built went on to win three consecutive Champions Leagues, a run unprecedented in the competition since Bayern Munich in the early 1970s. Obviously these were not my wins. But who is to say they would not have happened if I were still there?

The enforced break came at the most suitable time for me. For a while I had been suffering from cervical stenosis. I'd felt a tingling sensation in my hands, and I was advised that if I delayed treatment any longer it could spread to my legs. The symptoms were caused by a condition in which the spinal canal is too small for the spinal cord and nerve roots. I made an appointment to have an operation to widen the canal and planned to be out of the game for a while. I didn't know how long the recuperation would take. Of course, there were temptations to return at once. I had a conversation with Galliani at Milan about going back to my old job. The club had finished tenth in Serie A. Berlusconi was keen. It was hard to say no but I decided to have the surgery instead. It also gave me time to recharge my batteries.

By October I was starting to feel ready to get back into the fray. There is something about the job of managing a football club that is addictive and it is my drug of choice. This had also happened after I left Milan. I said I'd take some time off but then the season restarts and games from

THE DREAM

all the big leagues are on television, and you miss being on the touchline. When I started out as a young and inexperienced coach at Reggiana, I remember making a promise to myself that I would do the job for five or six years and that would be it. Twenty years later I was 55 and not yet ready to retire.

I didn't know where the next opportunity would come from, but I was open-minded. My name was linked in the media to all sorts of clubs, some of them English. Manchester United was mentioned, and then Chelsea when José Mourinho's second spell there ended. I spent some of my time in Vancouver, where my wife and I have a home – watching games on the TV, yes, but also fishing. The only thing I knew was that I didn't want to take charge of a team midway through the season, as I had with Juventus and then Paris Saint-Germain. I wanted to begin at the beginning of the football year, with a club that felt like it has a project.

Before the end of the year the right project came up. Pep Guardiola announced that he would be leaving Bayern Munich at the end of the 2015–16 season. He had been there for three years and didn't want to renew his contract. I was approached. The challenge would be an interesting one. Of course I liked the idea of working in the Bundesliga. It was the only top European league that I had no experience of. And the chance to take part in the Champions League again was also attractive. Bayern had won it as recently as 2013 but Guardiola had not managed to win it in his spell there.

DER WANDERER, 2014–19

First, of course, I had to do a crash course in German, which was even harder to learn than English. When I arrived for my first press conference, I had done enough to manage a sentence or two, and then I carried on in English. To help me fit in, the club presented me with a pair of lederhosen on my arrival. To make myself feel more at home, I immediately hired Paul Clement to join me in Munich.

More than any of the clubs I had worked at around Europe, Bayern were the emperors of their league. They had won the Bundesliga for the four previous seasons, and that would continue long after I left. They finally released their grip in 2024, when Bayer Leverkusen won their first ever title, coached by none other than Xabi Alonso. But I'm getting ahead of myself. When I arrived in Munich Alonso was still playing, and I was pleased to see a friendly face. The club captain was Philipp Lahm, who led Germany to their World Cup win two years earlier. Among the club's other leading players were the keeper Manuel Neuer, the defenders Jérôme Boateng and David Alaba, the midfielders Arjen Robben, Thiago Alcântara, Joshua Kimmich and Franck Ribéry, and the strikers Thomas Müller and the prolific goalscorer Robert Lewandowski. That summer the squad was strengthened by the arrival from Dortmund of Mats Hummels. There was a lot of talent to choose from. The only potential worry was that it was an ageing team. Ribéry and Robben were well into their thirties, and Xabi Alonso and Lahm would both retire at the end of the season.

THE DREAM

At Real I had inherited a squad that had played under Mourinho for three years. For three years Bayern had played the Guardiola way. Very different! I didn't want to change much this time round. Attacking football is a tradition at Bayern and I wasn't about to interfere. But as usual I introduced a system that has worked for teams I coach wherever I travel. My philosophy was to mix discipline with freedom. So, when the opposition has the ball, defend in one of two ways only, a high press or a low block. Then when possession is gained, try to play forward quickly, more directly, more vertically. But when you get to the final third, everything changes. That's where you need creativity and freedom, because without it you only have sterile possession. This is especially true if your opponent's defence is organised.

It worked. There were some tired performances over the winter, and some very tight games. These prompted a certain amount of external noise and criticism. But by now I was nearly a thousand games into my coaching career and knew how to weather a storm. We ran away with the Bundesliga that season, winning it by 15 points, a bigger margin by five points than the two previous seasons under Pep. However, this was not considered to be success at Bayern. It was the least that was expected.

Whenever there was heat in the media, I noticed a big difference to this job. The thing that was completely new to me was the experience of working at a club that was not run according to the whims of one lone charismatic owner.

DER WANDERER, 2014–19

Instead, it had a mixed set of corporate shareholders, while the club itself was traditionally managed at the senior level by legendary ex-players. There was a change of president mid-season, with Uli Hoeness taking over. The chairman was Karl-Heinz Rummenigge, who had been at Inter Milan when I was at Roma. Did I kick my future boss when I played against him? Of course I did. That was my job.

So I was answerable to various significant individuals. It was difficult for me to know who wielded more power and after I'd been there for a few weeks I even took Philipp Lahm aside and asked for his opinion. But as ever I did my best to maintain my independence. There was one time when the bosses asked me to get the players to be more disciplined and issued me with a list of five bullet points to read out to them. My view was that the first team was not the youth team and should be treated as such. So I stood in the dressing room, took out the piece of paper and said, 'I have an order from the board to read you a list.' It was my way of distancing myself from the task.

Of course, even without the owner breathing down your neck, there is still the same pressure to succeed in the Champions League. My job was to win it. Just like Mourinho before me at Real, Guardiola had taken the club to three semi-finals on the trot. I had won it three times as a coach and now Bayern wanted me to do it for them.

For the first time in as long as I could remember, a club coached by me did not finish top of its group. The winner

THE DREAM

was Atlético. In the head-to-head games, both clubs won 1–0 at home. We beat PSV twice but managed to lose to Rostov. Still, we were through and, for the second time in my Champions League career, my side was playing Arsenal next. We were struggling to express ourselves in the Bundesliga at this point in the season, and as we entered the knockout phase there was expectation of a big performance. It turned out to be a massacre. We thrashed them 5–1 at home. Away at Highbury, they had a man sent off in the second half, and we put five past them again.

Then came Real Madrid. These clashes against your old club happen if you move around. In the 2003 final Milan played Juventus, who had sacked me two years before. Now my task was to plot the elimination of another club that had let me go. At least I knew the opposition well. The front three in the first leg was the famous trio, the BBC. In such situations, where you go back to an old club, it is crazy to say that it is just another game. That club was only recently your family, and your new family has to hurt your previous family. It was made more difficult for me because, with the corporate nature of the senior management, Bayern felt like less of a family in the first place.

We had a big misfortune just before the first leg. Lewandowski was injured in a league game against Dortmund. This was a blow, because he was a goal machine. By the end of the season, he had 43 in all competitions. Müller was not having a great time and had scored just one goal so far, but

DER WANDERER, 2014–19

I had no choice but to play him up front and hope his luck would change. But still we went one up when Arturo Vidal met a corner with a powerful header. Then on the stroke of half-time we won a penalty. In Lewandowski's absence Vidal stepped in and fired his shot wildly over the bar. A second goal could have put us in a strong position to defend our lead, so it was a bad miss. Ronaldo hadn't scored in six Champions League games but chose the start of the second half to break that run and volley in an equaliser. Then with half an hour to go Javi Martínez was sent off and Ronaldo stabbed in the winner. We played well, but Neuer also had to work very hard to keep us in the game.

I went back to Madrid for the biggest game I had been involved in for two years. This was enough of a personal drama for me to deal with, but then there was the drama out on the pitch. It must have been an incredible game for the neutral to enjoy. For everyone else, it was nerve-racking. At the Bernabéu we almost managed to do to them what they had done to us at the Allianz Arena. We began strongly and dominated the first half with energetic, sweeping football. I went into the tie knowing that Real score in every game, but concede in every game too, and that we had Lewandowski back. When we won a penalty early in the second half he buried it. As we pushed for a second to win the tie, Ronaldo headed them level with a quarter of an hour to go.

Almost at once Ramos accidentally gifted us an own goal. It was 3–3 on aggregate. Unfortunately, with only minutes

THE DREAM

left, Vidal completed his interesting contribution to the tie by getting sent off. To be honest it was an unjust second booking. We had not enough left in the tank to hold them, and at the end of the first half of extra time Ronaldo got two more. Both were clearly offside. With his hat-trick he scored his hundredth goal in the Champions League. And I thought we were friends! Asensio made it 6–3.

The sending-off turned the game. I felt we had been hard done by. Afterwards I suggested that the referee had not been up to the task of handling such an important game, and that the time had come to consider the introduction of video technology. I can't believe I suggested that.

What happened next was unexpected. We ran away with the Bundesliga and on the last home game of the season I was showered with Bavarian Weissbier. Over the summer we refreshed the squad by signing James Rodríguez on loan. Things had not been going well for him at Real and I was happy to have him. But some senior players in the squad were unhappy, Robben and Boateng among them. At the start of 2017–18 we stuttered a bit in the league, losing one game and drawing another. The Champions League campaign started positively with a 3–0 home win over Anderlecht. Then at the end of September we went to another of my old clubs. Against Paris Saint-Germain I decided to do without the two ageing wide players, and let our full-backs come forward while we focused on attacking through the centre. It was a mistake. The balance was wrong and it allowed their counter-attacking to kill us. They scored their first in the second minute. The 3–0 scoreline was Bayern's heaviest defeat in the competition for 21 years. The day after the game the club's board met and came to the conclusion that the problem was me.

'The performance of our team since the start of the season did not meet the expectations we put on them,' said Rummenigge. 'The game in Paris clearly showed that we had to draw consequences.'

I had now been let go four times by big clubs: Juventus, Chelsea, Real Madrid and Bayern Munich. It just goes to show that it doesn't take an erratic president or an unpredictable owner to drop the guillotine. Corporate shareholders can do the job too. This was the most ruthless sacking of my entire career. After I left, they managed to reach the semi-final and then got knocked out by – guess who? – Real Madrid.

In the meantime I now had another winter to get through and the chance to consider what to do next. There was speculation that I might be the right replacement for Arsène Wenger when his long tenure at Arsenal finally came to an end in May 2018. My name had been linked with Chelsea and Manchester United over the years too. I always return to Vancouver for recovery periods and that's where I received the offer to go to my next job, back home to Italy.

Napoli had a vacancy because Maurizio Sarri, after a contract dispute, had decided to leave and try his luck at

Chelsea. He had done well in Serie A, finishing second, third and second. But the club's results had been disappointing in Europe, which is maybe why they turned to me.

I was not quite able to change the narrative, though I got close. We were second in Serie A for almost all of the season, and finished behind Juventus, who were on a long run of winning the Scudetto year after year. Meanwhile Napoli was drawn in a tough Champions League group with PSG, Liverpool and Red Star Belgrade. Unlike at other clubs I'd been at, I wasn't taking over a squad full of superstars. Most of the talent was up front with Lorenzo Insigne and Dries Mertens. To get through the group would be a miracle, but we almost managed it.

Perhaps our most costly result was a draw away to Red Star in the opening game. But there was also a tough lesson when we went to Paris. We were winning 2–1 until the last minute, when Di María took a pass on the edge of the box and with his left foot curled a shot into the corner. As he shaped up on his left foot I thought, *I've seen this video clip before*, and sure enough it sailed in, a glorious finish. We drew with them at home too.

The big task was to try and get the better of Liverpool. We talked about it a lot and came up with a plan to bypass the high press that they worked so well under Jürgen Klopp. In our first game against them, at home, the very first time we had possession we launched a long ball from our goalkeeper towards their left back, Andy Robertson, who was not so tall. It worked in driving their press backwards and holding them at bay. We won with a last-minute winner and went to Anfield in the last game knowing that we needed to score, and not lose by two clear goals, in order to progress. Unfortunately, two moments of world-class brilliance did for us: a goal by Mo Salah slipping in through the inside left channel, and a last-minute block by Alisson, who had recently become the most expensive goalkeeper in transfer history. 'If I knew Alisson was this good, I would have paid double,' Klopp joked. Liverpool went on to win the competition.

I had not been eliminated at this stage since 1999. There was a chance for revenge the following season when we were drawn against Liverpool again in the same group. They came to the Stadio San Paolo and we beat them with two late goals. It was an easier group, and we qualified for the knockout stage in second place. A respectable result. Unfortunately, things were not going so well in Serie A. We were loitering in seventh place and had not won a game in a while when, the morning after we won our sixth group game 4–0, I was asked to come and have dinner with the club president, the film producer Aurelio De Laurentiis. Whatever tactical errors I may have made as a coach, I now think that one of the biggest mistakes of my career was accepting that invitation. I knew that he was going to sack me and there was absolutely no need to go and receive the news in person. I should have gone home and waited for the phone to ring. It was an uncomfortable meal.

THE DREAM

'I remain his friend, I was before and I still am now,' said the president in a statement. 'I am sorry that things have gone like this. We have cultivated a dream but suddenly awakened. It was better that everyone went their own way.' The next day Gennaro Gattuso, my old midfield battler at Milan, entered the club through the revolving door. I was not happy with him as he seemed to have been waiting behind that door without warning me.

Statistically my time at Napoli was my least successful in coaching. But I felt I'd left them in a good place. In the round of 16 they were drawn against Barcelona and after the home game in late February the tie was poised at 1–1.

Then came Covid.

15

THE SIXTH TIME, 2019–22

Things can move fast in football. I was an out-of-work 60-year-old and a paid-up member of one of the world's biggest and least exclusive clubs: the sacked managers' club.

That's the age at which most coaches have retired from the grind of the week-in week-out schedule and walked away from the pressure to get result after result, but my curse is that I found it hard to walk away. I needed to be in football. In the middle of the season there are always clubs in trouble and looking to make changes and rather than be idle at home I decided to listen to offers. At the time two big English clubs were in trouble. Arsenal had fired their manager, and Everton had done the same, and both first teams were being run by caretakers. As I had just become a free agent, perhaps unsurprisingly my name came up in connection with both jobs.

I can't deny that Arsenal would have been an attractive challenge. I still owned property in London. But I had good intelligence that they were going to appoint Mikel Arteta. So I listened instead to the overture coming from Everton, who offered me a four-and-a-half-year contract. All this less than a month since I had brought Napoli to the city and got a 1–1 draw with Liverpool in the Champions League.

The first game I watched from the stands happened to be against Arsenal. Goodison Park held a particular memory for me. It was here, after the last game of the season in 2011, that I was sacked in the corridor by the Chelsea CEO. We didn't win that day or on any of the other times I sent out a team against them during my time in England. Three draws, three defeats. I knew from personal experience that this was a club with pride and history, and I made it clear that we must make it our goal to qualify for the Champions League.

It was good to be back in England. If I could put a finger on why I like it there so much, I'd say it's because the stadiums are full, and there is always drama and excitement. It is tribal and that seems to make it different to other leagues. Maybe in a relatively small country it is easier for fans to travel to away games and that contributes to the atmosphere, which is completely different in English stadiums. The fans have a passion that rarely expresses itself in violence and insult. I have never been insulted in an English stadium, as I have often been in Italian ones.

The Premier League is hectic. I was soon pitting my wits against Pep Guardiola. In the FA Cup I went back to Anfield, where Everton had not won a game in the twenty-first

THE SIXTH TIME, 2019–22

century. In March I politely queried a goal disallowed by VAR that would have given us a last-minute win over Manchester United, and the ref sent me off. Then I went back to Chelsea for the first time, who were managed by my friend Frank Lampard.

And this was just my first couple of months. After that, all normal life was put on pause when COVID-19 struck and we entered a pandemic. Like everyone else, I couldn't go far. Usually I like to find a home in the heart of the city where I work, but in England's north-west I lived in Crosby, a coastal suburb of Liverpool. There I was able to walk on the beach and count the hundred iron statues made by the sculptor Antony Gormley, which disappeared every time the tide came in. Sometimes I bumped into my neighbour Jamie Carragher when he was walking his dog. I cycled a lot and found some good rides from Crosby to Southport. I really enjoyed the place, and it helped that the weather was good. I have to admit that I felt lucky and slightly guilty to be able to live relatively normally during the pandemic.

Football played its part responsibly. At Everton the senior staff all accepted wage cuts and deferrals so that the club could pay the salaries of less well-rewarded staff. And when we were allowed to resume, it felt good to put a smile back on the faces of supporters who wanted to be reconnected with their club. There was a special smile for Everton fans in our first game back. If we lost at home to Liverpool, there was a chance they would win the title for the first time in

THE DREAM

30 years. For them to win the title at Goodison, even without any fans in the stadium to witness it, would have been unacceptable. We managed to ensure they had to win the title somewhere else, although I did send Klopp a congratulatory text.

We finished in 12th place, three places higher than when I joined at Christmas. It was clear that the squad needed strengthening. The biggest player at Everton was the England goalkeeper Jordan Pickford, and there were good strikers in Richarlison and Dominic Calvert-Lewin. There was very little break between the end of one season and the start of the next and I used it to recruit two former players: Allan, the Brazilian who played as a defensive midfielder at Napoli, and James Rodríguez from Real Madrid. Abdoulaye Doucoure joined from Watford. Also, and perhaps my best bit of business, was to OK getting Jarrad Branthwaite back from Carlisle United as soon as I arrived. He had been at our academy but was maturing fast at Carlisle and £1 million was good value. I was certain that he had a big future ahead of him.

Things had not gone so well for Rodríguez, partly owing to injury, but partly because he was seen as a bit of a luxury by some coaches. I liked him and wanted to help him help Everton. My new recruits started very well. We won our first four games and were top of the table. Then we drew with Liverpool in a very controversial and heated game. By the end of the year, we were still in second place, as high as Everton had been at Christmas in many decades. I still thought

THE SIXTH TIME, 2019–22

the title was beyond us, but it was not unrealistic to aim for Champions League qualification.

The one thing I was able to deliver to Everton fans was their first win over Liverpool since 2010, and their first win at Anfield since 1999. But we became complacent against the lower teams, and we slipped down to tenth. As the season came to a close, I challenged some of the players who I thought were not as motivated as they should be. If they wanted to leave, they could and they should. I would go and find replacements who could make a more positive contribution. It was in search of such players that I got on the phone to Real Madrid, asking if they had anyone who I could take on loan. And the conversation went in an unexpected direction.

The answer was that they didn't. Obviously, everyone knew that they were also in the market for a new manager since Zidane had resigned for the second time, citing a lack of support from the club. To replace him they had lined up Massimiliano Allegri, who had won so many Scudetti at Juventus and led them to two Champions League finals. But at the last moment he decided to remain at Juventus. The voice on the other end of the line complained that there were no coaches out there.

'If no players,' I said, 'could you use a new manager?'

'Do you know anybody?' came the response.

'Do you not remember what we did in 2014?' I responded.

There was a silence.

THE DREAM

'Maybe. I'll speak with the president and get back to you.'

The next day I was on a train when my phone rang. I looked at the screen and saw that it was Florentino Pérez. My first thought was, *Please don't let the train go into a tunnel now.* It didn't and we spoke. In ten minutes, the deal was done. It was a Saturday. I went to my director of football at Everton and explained the situation. The club was a bit stunned because everyone assumed, me included, that I would stay at Everton for the three years remaining on my contract. But that is football. Coaches rarely get to decide when they leave a job – I certainly didn't at Real – so they shouldn't be criticised when they do. This was too good an opportunity to ignore. The two clubs quickly agreed compensation and, three days after I spoke to the president, I was presented to the Spanish media.

It was a remarkable turn of events for me. I had been in football since 1977, more than 45 years, and I had been coaching for 30 of them. Having wandered the continent for six years, now I was going back to the most famous club of them all. But as I made my way to the training ground for pre-season, the squad had a familiar look. Ramos and Varane had just left, but many players were still there. The likes of Casemiro, Isco, Carvajal, Kroos and Nacho, who had all been given their first start in the team by me, were now long established, while Benzema, Modrić and the captain Marcelo were all well into their thirties but still vital members of the side. It was back to the future. There were the

THE SIXTH TIME, 2019–22

same physios, the same kit men, as well as the same journalists asking the same questions. And the same object as ever. Play attacking football. Score a lot of goals. Win games. Win titles. Win the Champions League, again and again. It felt like coming home.

For the first ten games or so, I was trying to work out how best to integrate the young guns with the old guard. The rising stars who were already there included the Brazilians Vinícius Júnior and Rodrygo, and they were now joined by Eduardo Camavinga. New defensive signings since my previous time in Madrid were Éder Militão and David Alaba, who I knew from Bayern. Sadly, I had less success getting the best out of Eden Hazard, a great talent, who had been suffering from injury since arriving at Real. Gareth Bale, too, who was back after a loan spell with his old club Spurs, was unable to get back to top form. Opportunities for them were limited because Vinícius was quickly becoming irreplaceable. He was clearly en route to being one of the best players in the world, if not the best.

We won El Clásico in late October and soon established ourselves at the top of La Liga. In December we won the derby with Atlético – the first time I'd managed to get the better of Diego Simeone in the league. In the meantime, I made my return to the Champions League with an away win at the San Siro against Inter Milan. It was an open game with a lot of chances. We took ours with only a minute to go. Fede Valverde lifted a pass into the box and Camavinga volleyed the ball into the path of Rodrygo, who swept it into the corner. It was a beautiful way to start our campaign, and it came via the youngest players in the side. Camavinga was only 19 and Rodrygo 20.

The group matches were predictable and we achieved our objective of progressing fairly easily, with one notable exception, which turned out to be a very ugly wake-up call. It was an emotional night when European football returned to the Bernabéu after a project of renovations that had lasted nearly two years. Our visitors were Sheriff Tiraspol, the Moldovan champions who had come through four qualifying rounds to reach the group stage for the first time. Dirk Kuyt, the former Liverpool player who was now a pundit, didn't do us any favours by saying on Dutch TV that 'teams like Sheriff Tiraspol have nothing to do with the Champions League'. They were out to prove him and others wrong. They had already beaten Shakhtar Donetsk in their opening fixture, so were not the massive underdogs they were made out to be.

Sheriff defended stoutly, and apart from two spectacular moments for the Moldovans the game was all Madrid – to the extent that Sheriff's on-loan keeper Georgios Athanasiadis won UEFA's Player of the Match award. It was our first defeat of the season. I was not so much worried as disappointed. We played with intensity and commitment and had total control but lost due to the finest details. The team played well; we could have been sharper with our finishing but it's difficult to explain what happened. You could say we had bad luck. They scored their goals on the counter-attack and from a throw-in. We had a lot of shots at goal but sometimes luck deserts you in games. Everything went well for them; everything went badly for us.

The referee didn't have such a great game, missing a couple of penalties. He did eventually award us one, enabling Benzema to equalise the header they scored against the run of play in the first half. Then in the 89th minute – exactly when we got a winner against Inter – Sheriff got one against us. A half-clearance reached Sébastien Thill, a Luxembourg international who was unmarked on the edge of the box, and he thumped a half-volley with his left foot into the top corner. We played with intensity and commitment, but the small details cost us the game. We had two-thirds of the possession, 30 shots, 13 corners and scored once from the spot. They had no corners, only four attempts and scored two. It was proof of how difficult things can be against the so-called weaker teams.

The other result of note in the group phase was an away victory at Shakhtar Donetsk because it challenged the dogma of the high press. Coached by Roberto De Zerbi, they were a very good team. What he was doing with full-backs, and other positions, was really interesting. I instructed my players not to press, because that's what they wanted us to do. 'If you press,' I said, 'they will pass the ball around you. Don't press, and they will give the ball to you.' We didn't press – and we won 5–0.

THE DREAM

After an own goal in the first half, in the second the key goals came from the youngsters. Two were scored by Vinícius, the second with an amazing dribble; he then put in a perfect pull-back for Rodrygo to score. Benzema broke Shakhtar's offside trap to add a fifth in injury time. He got two more against them at home. Next, we went to Moldova and beat Sheriff 3–0. Finally Inter came to Madrid for the decider to see which of us would top the group. We got a satisfying, dominant win that mixed teamwork and individual brilliance. For our first, Rodrygo drove the ball low across the box towards Casemiro, who heard a call from behind and stepped over it, leaving an unmarked Kroos to drive a shot into the far corner. In the second half Asensio's goal was even better. From the other corner of the box, he drove a fantastic shot into the top corner.

This team that I had inherited was missing certain talismans from my last stint at the club. Ronaldo was gone, as were Ramos and Casillas. But without them their successors were developing their own identity. Thibault Courtois, previously at Chelsea and Atlético, was a huge presence in goal and would develop, in my opinion, into the best goalkeeper in the world. Benzema, as the only surviving member of the BBC trio – Bale was not able to play many games on his return – assumed a new responsibility as a leader and senior player surrounded by much younger team-mates. No longer operating as a hard-running foil and support for Ronaldo and Bale, he rose to the challenge of being the focal point of

THE SIXTH TIME, 2019–22

our attack. At the age of 34, he had the energy and hunger of someone ten years younger, and his influential role as we entered the knockout phase made all the difference.

There was also a major rule change as we reached the round of 16. The away goals rule had been scrapped. It was introduced in the 1960s to encourage away teams to attack more, but UEFA decided that nowadays it had actually tended to put a brake on home teams, who were more concerned with not conceding than with scoring. I acknowledge that was also probably true of myself. Under the new rule, if ties were level after the second leg, then teams would go straight to extra time and a penalty shoot-out if required. It no longer mattered who had scored more goals away from home. If it was 4–4 in one leg and 0–0 in the other, there was no longer an advantage in scoring all those away goals. This required a change in mentality. There was no need to be so cautious at home anymore.

As we played through the winter towards the spring, our starting eleven was reaching the sort of stability that is needed to compete across both La Liga and the Champions League. It mirrored the balance between disciplined defensive control and the freedom of attacking creativity that is at the heart of my simple – but hopefully not simplistic – approach to the game. The pace of our front players enabled the counter-attack to be our best weapon. Just as important was the solid defensive base from which to launch those counter-attacks. When we had the ball, the formation

THE DREAM

consisted of a back four screened by a defensive midfielder, and in front of them there would be two midfielders feeding three front players. But out of possession, whoever was on the right would tuck back into midfield.

The knockout stages are where the real pressure begins. A performance like the one against Sheriff cannot be remedied; the dream would be dead. In the last 16 we came up against an in-form PSG during an indifferent run of their own. If you've been in the game as long as I have, and managed as many clubs as I have, the chances of being drawn to play against a former employer are quite high. It had happened to me before, of course, but there was an extra sense of drama when the draw pitted us against Paris Saint-Germain. They had been very busy in the transfer market since my time there.

To beat them we were going to have to overcome a trio of *galácticos* that had been assembled exactly for ties like this – Mbappé, Neymar, Messi. On paper, MNM was just as formidable as BBC. In fact, Neymar was on the bench for the first leg in Paris, but that didn't stop PSG dominating every statistic at the Parc des Princes. Somehow we managed to get out of Paris with only a one-goal deficit. While we had very few chances, they had many more, but Courtois was equal to them all. He is a man-mountain and very difficult to beat. Messi couldn't do it from the penalty spot. Mbappé was stopped by two great saves. It was only in the fourth minute of injury time, when Neymar backheeled the ball into his path, that Mbappé burgled his way from the left wing into the box through two defenders and drove a shot into the corner. Even then we might have survived as Courtois' outstretched leg was only beaten by the tiniest nick off Valverde that sent the ball between the goalkeeper's legs.

What was not acceptable was that we had been unable to break out of PSG's high press. We couldn't get out with the ball, and we misplaced a lot of passes. In the second leg we would need to work harder in every phase of the game and be much better on the ball. I had to make some adjustments to selection because Casemiro, the steady metronome at the heart of midfield, was suspended. So I selected Kroos to play the holding role flanked by Modrić and Valverde with Asensio and Vinícius playing either side of Benzema.

The game did not start well, and it quickly got worse. Before we had made much headway Mbappé had put the ball in the net three times. Luckily, two of them were offside. The one that counted came from a Neymar assist, who chipped a pass forward for Mbappé to run on to and beat Courtois at the near post.

However, the players did do what I had asked: they ran further, had more goal attempts, more turnovers, more tackles and all from less possession and close to 150 fewer passes than their opponents, and with that we reversed all our statistics from the first leg.

We were two down in the tie with half an hour to go when Benzema stepped up for us and took control of the game.

THE DREAM

Since the departure of Ronaldo and with fewer contributions from Bale in his final Madrid season, Benzema had assumed a leader's role in the front line. This new and freer role also allowed him to become a more prolific goalscorer himself, which was another key component to the team's success. This all happened without my intervention. Somehow it just came about, almost organically, from him as he gave expression to his own personality. The young players, especially Vinícius and Rodrygo, seemed to look naturally to him, and he enjoyed their respect. I would like to take credit for this, but it all came from the players. My contribution was not to interfere.

The game changed when, like a terrier, Benzema chased down a long, lazy backpass to their keeper, Gianluigi Donnarumma, who was caught dawdling. He should have kicked it out for a corner but instead he passed across the goal. Vinícius was waiting and pounced on the ball, calmly playing it inside to Benzema.

Then with 15 minutes left Benzema rapidly completed a hat-trick as Vinícius terrorised the PSG defence. First Modrić ran from inside his own half, virtually unchallenged, through a gaping hole in the PSG midfield and fed Vinícius in the inside left channel. Vinícius jinked and feinted and drew defenders towards him before sliding a pass back to Modrić. Modrić slipped a deft short pass to Benzema, who, taking a single touch, spun through 180 degrees and fired home. Twelve seconds after the restart, Vinícius received the ball in the inside left channel. The PSG captain, Marquinhos, intercepted the ball but his head must have been a bit scrambled by our comeback because he passed it straight into the path of Benzema. It took just 16 minutes to end PSG's Champions League dream for another year. Benzema 3, PSG 1.

I was more confident that Real could have the beating of the next old club that the draw threw at me: Chelsea, now managed by Thomas Tuchel. But it is important at this point to step away from the normal narrative of football to recall that the Russian invasion of Ukraine took place in February 2022. The continent of Europe became a more insecure place. The most immediate impact in footballing terms was the fact that Roman Abramovich was forced to step away from his running of Chelsea, and soon after that he was made to terminate his ownership. Against this backdrop of what must have been a difficult time within the Chelsea organisation, Real went to Stamford Bridge and we tried to focus on the task in hand. We had just lost El Clásico in humiliating fashion: a 4–0 drubbing at home. So the club needed us to respond.

Another Benzema hat-trick was the best medicine. The understanding between him and Vinícius was deepening with every game, and soon they were tearing through the Chelsea defence, where Antonio Rüdiger and my old PSG captain Thiago Silva, now 37, were desperately trying to stop them. Casemiro was back so Valverde was able to move to

THE DREAM

the right in front of Modrić, who, with Vinícius again, did a lot of the damage. Benzema got two incredible headers in the first half, one a thunderbolt, the other softer and subtler but just as deadly. Kai Havertz pulled one back for Chelsea before half-time, but straight after the break Benzema pounced on a disastrous error by their keeper, Mendy, who advanced out of his box and allowed Karim to roll his shot into an empty goal. To be honest, it could have been closer but for a couple of excellent saves by Courtois against his old club.

The way we were playing, with great efficiency, was beginning to become a pattern – a good pattern. When we looked at the numbers we found that with roughly equal amounts of possession Chelsea managed twenty goal attempts to our eight, but our finishing was much more accurate. Or, in other words, Benzema was the difference. In any previous season, his three away goals would have virtually guaranteed that we would have gone through. After all, who would back Chelsea to score three times away at the Bernabéu?

But remember Sheriff Tiraspol? Anything can happen in this competition, and it nearly did that night. Sometimes you can be caught in the no-man's land between protecting a lead and playing your normal attacking game, and that's where we seemed to have landed. We probably should have been much more aggressive but were taken by surprise. I admit this was my mistake. I should have been clearer in my instructions. Instead we allowed Chelsea to dominate from the outset. They surprised us by jumping into a lead through Mason Mount after only 15 minutes. A Rüdiger header levelled the tie straight after half-time. Then with 15 minutes left a mazy dribble from Timo Werner put them 4–3 in front on aggregate. The tables had been completely turned.

It seemed to me as if we didn't have the hunger to finish them off at home because we thought that we'd already done it away. We were the clinical team in front of goal in the first leg. Now it was them. Fortunately, they missed just enough chances to keep us in the tie, and somehow going three down liberated our team. The fans sensed it. They started to push, and the stadium did its magic. And so the story had yet another twist.

As soon as I could after the Werner goal, I introduced Rodrygo for Casemiro and two minutes later the tie was levelled on aggregate. Alaba cut out N'Golo Kanté's forward chip, allowing Marcelo to feed Modrić, who looked up and saw Rodrygo waiting at the edge of the box just beyond Thiago. And then one of those moments that only great players can produce happened. Modrić played an outrageous cross with the outside of his right foot that Rodrygo calmly volleyed home. As an ex-player I do not think that such a level of talent, necessary for the Modrić pass, should be allowed; it's just not fair on the rest of us ordinary players.

THE DREAM

We went into extra time. Six minutes in, Camavinga jumped on a misplaced pass out of Chelsea's defence and released Vinícius down the left, who crossed for Benzema to finish the tie as he began it, with an unstoppable header. It was his 38th goal of the season. We had lost the game 3–2 but won the tie 5–4.

Again, our efficiency, or maybe Chelsea's profligacy, had been decisive. Despite less possession and fewer goal attempts than the opposition, the results against PSG and Chelsea were not accidents. Our game plan had succeeded. It may not be the most expansive system, but it works and was the sensible tactic in knockout competition with the players we had. Staying in the game *is* the game. Winning is the objective.

I suffered a lot in that second leg. There is a remarkable piece of documentary film taken in the dressing room after that match which shows just how exhausting a game it was to be part of. It shows what all managers have to go through practically every game at the elite level. You live every moment, every error, every bit of bad luck, every reverse. You feel these things in your nervous system. And the relief and joy when things go your way are hard to measure. In the film I am slumped on a bench and looking pretty shabby. I puff out my cheeks and mumble, 'Dead. I'm dead. Incredible, incredible. If I don't die today, then I must be immortal. But what an atmosphere, right?'

I had a right to look exhausted. That Benzema goal made me the first coach to reach the Champions League

THE SIXTH TIME, 2019–22

semi-final in four separate decades. The oldest player in the Juventus side that lost to Manchester United in 1999 was Didier Deschamps, born in 1968. The youngest player in the Madrid team was Camavinga, born in 2002. That statistic alone shows how long I'd been trying to win this competition. But here's another. Nils Liedholm, my coach when Roma got to the final in 1984, was born in 1922!

But it was not considered a success at Real to get this far and go no further. Any sense of relief I felt at surviving two such topsy-turvy games was short-lived. The semi-final took us back to England, where Manchester City waited. They had become the new power of English football since the arrival of Pep Guardiola from Bayern Munich. I decided that the energy of Valverde was more important than the control of Casemiro. Kroos could do the holding role, which enabled Valverde to move to the right with Rodrygo ahead of him to stifle the threat of Bernardo Silva and Foden.

The good news was that once again we came to a top Premier League club and scored three goals. The less good news was that we conceded four. Kevin De Bruyne got the party started after only two minutes with a diving header. Gabriel Jesus made it two within ten. We were too soft, and it was a very poor start. Phil Foden and Riyad Mahrez were cutting us up on each flank and they had several more chances before Benzema – who else? – dragged us back into the tie with an opportunistic volley.

THE DREAM

This initiated a game of end-to-end, basketball-style football that was as exciting as it was exhausting. Foden was the first to score in the second half, restoring Man City's two-goal lead with a header. Two minutes later and we had replied through a Vinícius solo effort. What a run. He left Fernandinho for dead on the halfway line with one of his trademark feints, rolling the defender on the outside without ever touching the ball. He raced, unchallenged, all the way into the six-yard area to slip the ball past Ederson.

It was a stunning goal fit for such a dramatic game. Then they made it 4–2. After Oleksandr Zinchenko was upended, we were guilty of waiting for the whistle and allowed Bernardo Silva to play on, driving into the box and beating Courtois at the near post. As if the contest could not get any crazier, with less than 10 minutes left the referee spotted a handball in their box. Of course, the last word had to go to Benzema. The calmest man in the stadium, he stepped up and, as Ederson dived to his left, he dinked a soft chip into the middle of the net, Panenka-style. This only two weeks after he had missed two penalties in the same single league match. 4–3.

We were still in with a chance in the tie, despite enjoying only 40 per cent possession, almost entirely thanks to our efficiency in front of goal – the rest was thanks to Benzema. As with the usual analyses of Madrid matches in the Champions League, the numbers were revealing. Interestingly, one statistic stood out from that first-leg game: the distance covered. At this level there is rarely a great difference between elite teams, but City players covered 123 kilometres and Madrid only 115 kilometres. However, the *key* numbers again favoured the economy of Madrid.

With 60 per cent possession, City's conversion of goal attempts to on-target attempts was 30 per cent while Madrid's was 45 per cent with only 40 per cent possession. Madrid's efficiency in front of goal means that in virtually any situation we had a chance, especially with a tiring opposition and our electric pace in forward positions. Everybody knows that I may not be the greatest fan of statistics, but our efficiency pleases me, so I am happy to reference them.

As we waited for the second leg, something wonderful happened. We won La Liga with four games to spare by hammering Espanyol 4–0 at home. It was the earliest that Real had won it in 32 years, and it was the first time in 15 years that we had become champions in front of our own fans. It meant that I was able to make a unique claim – to have won the league championship in Italy, England, France, Germany and now Spain. The five major European leagues. That thing that is sometimes said about me – that I'm a cup coach who does less in league competition – looks a little harder to justify.

Though our confidence was boosted, there was not much time to dwell on our success. Four days later we had to find a way past Manchester City at the Bernabéu. It was another open game with the action switching up and down the pitch. But strangely there were no goals after 60 minutes, or 70, or 73. Then Mahrez was found in space on the right and curled an unstoppable shot inside the near post. 5–3. Suddenly we needed three goals to win. Or two just to stay in the tie and take it to extra time.

I took a decision that the path to the final lay with the youngsters. I had only just removed Kroos, but now I took off Casemiro and Modrić. The three of them had a combined age of 98. I replaced them with Camavinga, Rodrygo and Asensio, whose years added up to 66.

There were 15 minutes left. Fifteen minutes later there were zero minutes left and no goals from us. Then, with the Champions League slipping away, superman Benzema again came to our rescue. Camavinga lofted a diagonal cross from the right, clearing the last defender and reaching Benzema's left foot. He somehow managed to retrieve the ball before it went out of play and turned it back across the goal between City's Ruben Diaz and their goalkeeper, Ederson, both of whom paused for a mere fraction of a second – just long enough to allow Rodrygo to dart between them and bring us within one goal of City. We had one goal but still needed another with virtually no time left to play.

The stadium erupted and wanted more. We were now into injury time. Two minutes later Carvajal drove a flatter cross from the right into a crowd of defenders, only for Rodrygo to leap and glance a powerful header beyond

THE SIXTH TIME, 2019–22

Ederson. Incredibly, in two minutes we had drawn level in the tie.

They had more chances before the final whistle, but we somehow escaped. Now we had to play on. Five minutes into extra time, Benzema was tripped in the box. No Panenka this time. Instead, he drilled a low shot to the right corner and the keeper went the wrong way. He'd scored the winner at exactly the same time as he had done against Chelsea.

The moment that the Benzema penalty entered the goal I turned to Kroos and Marcelo on the sidelines to get their views on what to do now. Should I stick or twist? After the game the media would portray this as somehow extraordinary, but it felt perfectly natural to me. I don't believe in philosophies. I believe in the identity of the team, and the team had very senior players with good football brains. Kroos in particular felt like an extra member of the coaching staff, a bit like Paolo Maldini and Philipp Lahm had once been. 'We have all seen a few football games ourselves,' he said afterwards. 'That allows you to exchange ideas with the coach but, of course, in the end he decides, but naturally he's interested in our opinion.' If the experience is there, why wouldn't I use it? I listen before I decide, and I decide on the information in front of me.

The decision was to stick. I took off Benzema and sent on Dani Ceballos to hold the centre of midfield. With five minutes to go I took off two other tired players and sent on fresh legs. All of the old guard were now on the sideline, cheering on the kids as they held the line to the 120th minute. It felt exactly like the family I had back at Milan all those years ago, with the older brothers willing on their young siblings. And we made it. 6–5. In my first season back at Real Madrid, thanks to the heroics of Benzema in all three knockout rounds, and three vital goals at vital moments from Rodrygo, we were in the final.

I think we deserved to be. First of all because of our quality, but quality alone isn't enough in football at the elite level. Talent alone isn't enough. You have to combine that talent and come together to make a committed team. This club's history, its DNA, has pushed us forward in the tough moments thrown at us by the Champions League. If you keep coming back, it's because you have more than the opposition. With 17 minutes to go City were 5–3 up on aggregate; with two minutes to go they were still in front. By 90+1 they were heading for extra time. Five minutes later they were out. It was truly amazing but not surprising. Don't try to explain it other than to say, in football, anything can happen.

At Madrid, of course, it is not enough just to be in the final. It has to be won. And to do so we had to beat yet another club from the Premier League. This time it was Liverpool standing in our way. Liverpool, again. If you count the 1984 final in Rome, which I had to miss through injury, I had a long history of seeing them in the final. Istanbul 2005. Athens 2007. Now we would meet again at the Stade de France in 2022. For me there was the extra dimension that, until a year earlier, I had been manager of Liverpool's local rivals at Everton.

I had a lot of experience playing against Klopp's teams in Europe, first when he was at Dortmund, more recently when I was at Napoli and also at Everton in domestic competition. I had a decent record against him. The scene was set for a classic tactical battle with the Liverpool midfield, with Fabinho and Thiago Alcântara holding and Jordan Henderson breaking into forward positions, pitted against our possibly less mobile but more controlled Kroos, Casemiro and Modrić. The winners of that battle would be able to feed the dynamic front runners that both sides possessed. Any one of these could decide the game.

It helps when you know how the opposition is going to play. Our job was to break their high press when in possession. When not in possession, we had to make sure that their front three of Mo Salah, Sadio Mané and Luis Diaz could not get behind us. This meant playing with a low block and Valverde working as a fourth midfielder when we were out of possession. His other job was to shut down Virgil van Dijk's right foot before it could launch long diagonal cross-field passes to Salah on the right. Meanwhile up front Vinícius would hold the width, and Benzema would drop short to pick up the ball from the midfield.

We went into the game as underdogs. That sounds strange to say about Real Madrid, but Liverpool had enjoyed

THE DREAM

a dominant campaign. They won their group with maximum points, then swept aside Inter, Benfica and Villareal. They'd had no dramas on the way to the final and, sure enough, they dominated the first half and Courtois had to be at his best to keep holding them off.

I was not happy as we went into the dressing room at half-time. The midfield had never found its shape and as a result we were being beaten on every statistic except the main one, thankfully. The one plus point was their body language when Benzema, with our one shot on target, had a goal disallowed by VAR for offside. Before they noticed the assistant referee's flag their bodies slumped as if they feared that this would be the story of the game. Was there a hint of hesitation and even fear in their eyes? I hoped so.

We needed to move the ball more quickly and more vertically. We had to start the second half with more energy, to use the intensity of their press against them and then counter with the pace of Vinícius and the power of Benzema. On the hour it worked perfectly. Modrić sprang the trap. Receiving the ball 20 yards inside our half he conjured up a magical turn and played a reverse pass though the lines to Carvajal that broke the press. Carvajal transferred the ball to Casemiro and continued his own run forward. Casemiro moved it on to Valverde wide on the right who sped forward and, as Carvajal flew past him on the overlap, distracting Van Dijk for a crucial moment, Valverde spotted Vinícius advancing at the far post. He fired a low cross behind the retreating

THE SIXTH TIME, 2019–22

Liverpool back line where Trent Alexander-Arnold had lost sight of Vinicius coming in over his blind side shoulder and Vinícius had an easy side-foot finish. It was a true team goal, and our only shot on target in the half. But to realise the dream everybody has to play their part and at the other end of the pitch Courtois continued to be unbeatable. When Liverpool bought Alisson, they broke the world transfer record for a keeper. Madrid spent even more on Courtois. It was worth every cent.

I sent on young legs to relieve tiring older ones as the end approached. It's a measure of our strength in depth that the names of players left on the bench included Nacho, Bale, Hazard and our club captain Marcelo. The culture of the family within the club is important to me so I was delighted when, as the final whistle blew, Benzema passed the armband to Marcelo so that he could physically lift the trophy.

And so for the sixth time I got my hands on the cup. With that win, the unimaginable had happened. With two different clubs, I had now won the competition more than any other manager. More than Bob Paisley, more than Pep Guardiola, more than Zinedine Zidane. And I knew with absolute certainty that my job was safe for another year – maybe!

16

THE SEVENTH TIME, 2022–4

The next season was a strange one because it was interrupted mid-flow by the World Cup in Qatar. It was personally satisfying to win the Copa del Rey, the UEFA Super Cup and the FIFA Club World Cup. And because we had also won the Supercopa de España the previous year it meant that in two seasons this squad of players had lifted every club trophy possible. This was a rare achievement and one to be genuinely proud of.

As ever there were changes. We said goodbye to old friends – Marcelo, Bale, Isco and Casemiro. And we welcomed Aurélien Tchouaméni and Antonio Rüdiger. Sadly, we could not maintain any level of consistency. Although we won the first Clásico, we trailed in second place to Barcelona almost all season. In the Champions League, the group stage was finished a month earlier than usual to accommodate the repositioned World Cup. We emerged ahead of RB Leipzig, Shakhtar Donetsk and Celtic, then for the second season running we found ourselves up against the same three English clubs. The only difference was that Liverpool came first in the round of 16. We travelled to Anfield and went to sleep for the first 15 minutes, conceding two goals. Courtois made an incredibly rare error for the second, proving that he is human after all. Then we woke up and scored five, and followed that up with a 1–0 win at home.

In the quarter-final there was Chelsea. Frank Lampard was back in temporary charge of my old club, but they were in transition under new ownership after the departure of Abramovich. We beat them 2–0 at home and won the second leg by the same score. At the Bernabéu, to the amusement of the fans, I even did a bit of juggling when the ball came my way in the technical area. You never lose it.

The semi-final, played a month later than usual in May, was a repeat of the previous year, the second part of what would be a trilogy of matches against City. By the time we played it I had reached another personal landmark. I had now won more games in the Champions League than my friend Sir Alex Ferguson, who was the previous record holder. I really wanted to add a couple more victories before the season came to an end, but it was not to be. The score was 1–1 at the Bernabéu. It was a tense contest, and I thought we were better. But when we went back to the Etihad Stadium, they once again put four past us, but this time we had no answer. They completely controlled the entire game. We managed only 15 passes in the first 15 minutes. It was a really tough experience for us. Courtois kept out Erling Haaland with three brilliant saves, and Kroos hit the crossbar, but we didn't play with the courage and personality needed for games as big as this. They put a lot of pressure on us – much more than in the first leg – and we were unable to find solutions. I have to confess that Guardiola surprised me. We were expecting him to set up the side just as he had in the first leg, but he completely changed it. With Rodri and John Stones operating as a pair of holding midfielders, they played man to man and pressured us all over the pitch, but especially up front. Our plan to build from the back just couldn't function.

City went on to beat Inter in Istanbul and win the treble. A treble in any country is a fantastic achievement but especially so in England given the intensity of the league. It was a great validation of Guardiola's coaching abilities. In another season the president might well have decided to sacrifice me after failing to retain either La Liga or the Champions League. But perhaps he remembered that the last time he let me go, he later said that he regretted it. So I kept my job and, at the start of 2023–4, I was able to use the humbling by Manchester City as a motivational tool. The players had been humiliated at the Etihad and it had hurt.

In the 2023–4 season the team was changing face and the incoming players did not have the Etihad scars. For most of the season we lost Courtois to an ACL injury, so Kepa Arrizabalaga arrived on loan from Chelsea to provide back-up. Then he got injured and Andriy Lunin stepped up. And after so many years of commitment to Real, we lost Benzema to the Saudi league. That meant we were without two of the most important players from the unbeatable team that won in Paris 2022. In defence, both Éder Militão and Alaba were injured for much of the season too. So the team had to find new leaders and a new identity.

Perhaps the biggest change to the team was the arrival of the young English player Jude Bellingham from Borussia Dortmund. My task was to find a way of fitting him into the side. I decided to play him centrally as a quasi-number 10 in a 4–3–1–2 formation, or at the sharp end of a 4–4–2 diamond. As a holding midfielder I had Tchouaméni playing behind a combination of Camavinga, Valverde, Modrić and Kroos. Nacho became club captain in an experienced back four. As for the attack, I had the option of playing Vinícius and Rodrygo as a pair up front. Vinícius would stay on the left, where he was so damaging, and Rodrygo became the more central of the two. But the club also signed Joselu on loan. He might not have been a *galáctico*, but he gave us options. He was capable of changing the dynamic and acting as a closer replacement for Benzema.

Things went well from the beginning. Even though he was only 20, Bellingham slotted in perfectly and proved that he had the temperament to fill the white shirt and play with the confidence of a *galáctico*. When the season got under way, Bellingham just could not stop scoring. Four of his goals were winners scored in injury time. By October he'd

THE SEVENTH TIME, 2022–4

twice been named Player of the Month in Spain and by the end of the season he was named La Liga Player of the Year. We knew that he had the potential to be special but even we had not anticipated such an impact.

One of his more important goals was scored at the very end of our opening Champions League game against Union Berlin. They were debutants in the competition and rose to the occasion. It reminded me of when the Moldovan champions Sheriff Tiraspol came to the Bernabéu. As in that game, we dominated every statistic but couldn't break through. At least we managed to prevent them scoring and then in the fourth minute of injury time a shot from Valverde was blocked and bounced around like a pinball until it reached the feet of Bellingham. Goal! It wasn't his most beautiful goal of the campaign, but it was indicative of his predatory instincts. His most beautiful goal came at Napoli when he dribbled through traffic into the box and slid the ball past their keeper.

My return to Naples coincided with a strong run of form for Napoli and it was a see-saw affair. The first half produced three goals in 15 minutes, which began with Napoli going in front through an Østigård header after a mistake by our keeper, Arrizabalaga, who was replacing the injured Courtois. Then came two quick goals in reply by Vini Jnr and Bellingham. That put us in front, which is where we went into half-time.

Ten minutes into the second half and Napoli were level. Nacho blocked an attempted cross from Osimhen, which rebounded onto his arm. According to the laws at that time, it was a penalty, which was duly despatched by Napoli's Zielinski. On 78 minutes Valverde unleashed a shot from fully 25 yards that crashed against the crossbar, rebounded on the back of goalkeeper Meret's head and back into the goal – great shot, Valverde, unlucky, Meret.

Our next group game away to the Portuguese side Braga gave us three wins in a row with a 2–1 victory where the front three were the difference. Vinícius set up goals for Rodrygo and Bellingham, confirming the pattern of play that would not change, irrespective of the supporting players, while Vini Jnr was available to drive Madrid's attacking potency. Braga pulled a goal back soon after Bellingham's 61st-minute goal, and I shut up shop with some final-quarter defensive substitutions.

The good thing about our group games was that we started to see other players share the scoring duties. Brahim Díaz, who had returned from three seasons on loan to AC Milan, was a handy option to have up front. When Braga came to Madrid for the return match, he got one of several useful goals he scored that season, and we went on to win 3–0 and qualify for the next round. Napoli were next up at the Bernabéu and once again managed to get two against us, but we got four. In the frantic opening quarter, there was a superb curler from Rodrygo then a header from Bellingham breaking into space to meet a wonderful Alaba cross. In the last ten minutes the teenage midfielder Nico Paz scored from long range, and then Joselu finally managed to get on the scoresheet. This was a relief after several misses. I was pleased for him that he got two headers in Berlin and Dani Ceballos scored a last-minute winner to make it 3–2.

This was to be the very last year of the Champions League group phase. In 2024–5 a new format for the competition was to be introduced, and thus for the last time in a quarter of a century I stuck to my old plan of winning the early games then rotating the squad for the final two matches. In the sixth game, for example, Carvajal, Kroos, Camavinga, Vinícius, Mendy and Rüdiger all had the night off. Why take the chance when they would be needed later on in the competition?

Things were going well. By the end of the year, we had consolidated our position at the top of La Liga and we were to stay there for the rest of the season. The club hierarchy felt confident enough to offer me an extension to my contract for two years beyond the end of 2024. There had been talk in the press of me becoming the next coach of the Brazilian national team. Of course, such an opportunity would interest any football addict but once Madrid made their offer the Brazil talk stopped. Obviously, I know that these things are subject to results, but at that moment results were good, even with Bellingham missing with an injury for a few games near the start of 2024. Without him we still managed to win four in a row.

He wasn't fit for selection when we resumed our Champions League schedule with a round of 16 tie against RB

THE DREAM

Leipzig. Several defenders were also missing, but as ever my attitude was to focus my attention on the players who were available, not those who weren't. To plug the gaps in defence I put Tchouaméni in central defence with Kroos and Camavinga in central midfield, flanked by Valverde and Brahim. For most of the game we set ourselves up to play with a compact low block because we wanted to ensure Leipzig couldn't gain any advantage from our re-formed back line.

It was Brahim whose goal gave us a 1–0 win. At the start of the second half, he cut in from the right, jinked past two defenders and curled a left-footed shot around a third defender into the top corner. It was a fantastic goal, one which required not just skill but strength and determination. It earned us a hard-won victory, because Leipzig played with a lot of intensity and dominated the first half. Lunin was also able to show what strength in depth we had among our goalkeepers. He was outstanding, highly motivated and full of confidence.

When Leipzig came to us, Rüdiger and Bellingham were back and everyone expected the second leg to be relatively straightforward. It was anything but. At the end of a goalless first half, I decided to withdraw Camavinga and send on Rodrygo so that Bellingham had two players in front of him. It seemed to wake up the team. On 65 minutes Kroos intercepted a pass on the edge of our box and fed the ball to Bellingham, who drove up the centre of the pitch to the edge of Leipzig's box. He spotted a diagonal run into space from

THE SEVENTH TIME, 2022–4

Vinícius, slipped the ball into his path and with one touch we had completed the perfect counter-attack. It was especially pleasing for me because we had been working on getting Vinícius to venture into more central positions to receive the ball where he could finish with the least amount of touches.

Perhaps revelling in the beauty of the goal, we were caught out by an acrobatic Willi Orbán header within three minutes to level the match. As we couldn't afford to concede again, I made a couple of substitutions (Modric for Kroos and Joselu for Bellingham) to restore control and take the heat out of the game. It was not a great night, if I'm honest. We were nowhere near urgent enough while Leipzig played with nothing to lose. They had nearly twice as many goal attempts as we did. What mattered was that we were through to the quarter-finals.

The quarter-final felt like part three of a blockbuster trilogy as we faced Manchester City for the third time in three seasons. So far, the score was one semi-final win each. Although the clubs were to meet in the quarter-final this time, we went into the tie knowing that we were unlikely to encounter a more dangerous opponent later in the competition. And we were eager to gain revenge for the way we'd been embarrassed a year earlier.

Even though this was to be my 200th game as a coach in the Champions League, I was nervous at the thought of facing Guardiola again. But then I am always nervous in the hours before a game. The suffering continues during the

THE DREAM

games themselves. Only with victory can I get relief. In the days after a win, I am calmer again for a bit, but then the nerves start up once more and the suffering resumes. It's only when you win the actual tournament that there is genuine happiness – and relief. Suffering goes with the job. It's what keeps me alive. It's what gives me fuel.

My nerves weren't improved by the opening goal of the first leg at the Bernabéu. We were a goal down after barely a minute. Tchouaméni, still playing in central defence, brought down Jack Grealish and conceded a free kick 25 yards out. The resulting yellow card ruled him out for the second leg. The free kick seemed far enough out not to need more than a one-man wall. Bernardo Silva stepped up and bent a cunning low shot inside Lunin's near post to prove that, if you need a wall, one man is not enough.

It turned into one of those games, the kind you never plan for or foresee. It was always a clash of styles between my teams and Guardiola's. It can result in a game where the two sides cancel each other out. But sometimes the game just goes crazy. That's what happened here. Within ten minutes we were in front. Camavinga surged in from the left and his shot caught a deflection off Rúben Dias to go in past their keeper. Two minutes later and Rodrygo sped past Akanji down the left and bore down on goal with Akanji in his wake, Diaz desperately trying to cover his colleague and Ortega advancing from his goal to shut down Rodrygo's options. A fraction of a second before the three City players converged on him, Rodrygo calmly rolled the ball past them all, with a slight touch from Akanji's heel, and gently over the line. 2–1 to Madrid. Two goals in two minutes, and our noses were in front. It was quite a bad-tempered match, a sign that both sets of players now knew each other too well and felt a strong sense of rivalry. But there was also great quality. In the second half the next three goals were all scored from distance, each more spectacular than the last. First Foden received a short pass on the edge of the box and nudged the ball to his left to whip a brilliant shot into the top corner. Five minutes later there was an even better strike from Joško Gvardiol. We stayed a goal down until, with ten minutes to go, Valverde scored the best goal of the lot, running onto a Vinícius cross and volleying an unstoppable low drive from the right. 3–3.

It's never good to draw the first leg if it's at home, especially when the second leg would be against a Manchester City side that had not lost at home in the Champions League for six years. But I genuinely felt that we were in with a chance because the teams were so evenly matched. The only change I made was to bring back Nacho in central defence and send out probably our strongest available side to play a low block. It wasn't my usual choice, because I had the players who were capable of being much more attacking, but I saw that it was the best way to compete and win against a side who had put four past us at the Etihad two seasons running.

THE DREAM

The plan was to resist the temptation to press, because that's what City wanted. They were at their most effective against a side that pressed them. They were less sure if you didn't, and that's how they could end up giving you the ball. We'd tried a similar tactic against Shakhtar some years ago and scored in five counter-attacks, so it was at least worth a try.

The game settled into its by now routine pattern, but we were able to land the first punch with our first real attack on 12 minutes. A long high clearance found Bellingham just beyond the centre circle. He pulled the ball out of the sky with immaculate control and released Valverde, who played Vinícius in on the right. His low cross found Rodrygo, whose shot rebounded back off the keeper, Ederson, giving him a second chance to score.

The goal provoked a sustained City assault. For the next hour Lunin had all the answers to everything they could throw at him until Doku was sent on and created the opportunity for De Bruyne to equalise from close range. Nothing else could separate the two sides despite many substitutions. The aggregate score after extra time was 4–4. It was our turn to be thankful for the removal of the away goals rule. Now I was to be involved in a penalty shoot-out for the first time in several seasons.

It was 40 years since I'd watched Roma lose to Liverpool on penalties in the final. Some things never change. You never can tell who is going to miss. Who would have guessed that Modrić, who went first for us, would see his shot saved?

THE SEVENTH TIME, 2022–4

Rüdiger, on the other hand, went last and drove his penalty into the corner with confidence. One thing definitely has changed in all those years. The clubs do more preparation, and this time it worked for us. Our goalkeeping coach Luis Llopis became a specialist at studying opposition penalty takers. In a previous game he'd noticed that a certain player tended to go down the middle with his penalties. He told this to Lunin, but when Lunin came to face this player in a game he dived to one side. Sure enough, the ball went down the middle. In the locker room, Luis went crazy. 'Why did you do that?' he shouted. 'Why?' Lunin started to reply, 'I thought . . .'. 'Don't do that,' interrupted Luis, 'just listen to the research.'

Now Lunin listened when Luis gave him more research. He told him something he had discovered about Bernardo Silva. During normal time he shot his penalties into the corner, but in shoot-outs he would go down the middle. The analysis worked. We told Lunin to stand still, and he did, and Silva chipped his penalty straight into his arms. The one penalty taker we couldn't prepare for was Ederson, the Man City goalkeeper. He stepped up because Haaland and De Bruyne had both been substituted and buried his penalty expertly in the corner. Mateo Kovačić's was also saved, while the rest of ours went in and we were through to the semi-final.

The truth is that I had a strong positive feeling that, once we got to the shoot-out, we would win. We defended very well and far deeper than we expected to. But in such a big game you need to fight to survive and sacrifice everything and we did, the way Real Madrid knows how to do. There was no other way to beat Manchester City, and I was very proud of the way that we managed it, neutralising their strengths and having a similar conversion rate for our shots on target despite enjoying less possession and making fewer passes.

By getting to the semi-final, I had equalled Pep Guardiola's record of reaching the Champions League semi-finals ten times as a manager. Seventeen days later we also secured La Liga – if we could win the Champions League, we would deliver the second half of a double.

It's always an interesting moment for me when the Champions League draw takes me back to an old club. Especially when that club is Bayern Munich. I did not depart on ideal terms and this little subplot is always in the background when I send out a side to play them. They were now being coached by Thomas Tuchel, although it was widely reported that after poor results in the Bundesliga he would not be returning the next season. I knew how he must be feeling!

Any side coached by Tuchel was capable of causing us problems, and that's exactly what happened in the opening phase of the first leg at the Allianz Arena. Bayern were all over us. They had already had seven shots before, midway through the half, Kroos sent a sublime pass through the heart of their defence for Vinícius to run on to and slide past Manuel Neuer. It was our first shot of the game. Tuchel

THE SEVENTH TIME, 2022–4

shifted things around at half-time, moving Leroy Sané onto the right flank. It coincided with us becoming more passive in defence, and it worked. After ten minutes he received a pass there, drove towards the box and shot hard inside Lunin's near post. Not long afterwards, Jamal Musiala was brought down by Lucas Vázquez and Harry Kane scored from the spot. They deserved their lead. With Bellingham tiring I decided to take him off and shake things up. Rodrygo burst into the box and now we had our own penalty, which Vinícius buried. It finished 2–2. I was proud that we managed to stay in the tie because we were second best. And before Bayern came back to the Bernabéu, I was also proud that we had secured La Liga again.

There was an interesting lesson for us in the second leg. Often a club as big as Madrid can spend many millions on a player in transfer fees and salaries. And sometimes it just doesn't work out. They can get injured, or their face doesn't quite fit, and all the hope the fans invested in them fades away. But in football the reverse is also true. There is always another humbler route to glory, and it doesn't involve a player arriving at the club with a big fanfare.

In the second semi-final, that player was Joselu. He started out at Real in 2011 but then went on a long journey that took him to Newcastle United and Stoke City in England. In the summer we had the chance to sign Harry Kane, but he went to Bayern. The only striker who arrived back in Madrid was Joselu, who came on loan from Espanyol in the

THE DREAM

second division. The two goals he scored in three minutes in the second leg were historic.

We needed both and we needed them fast because midway through the second half it was Bayern who scored first. The goal came through Alphonso Davies, who had come on as a sub in the first half. He'd never scored in the Champions League before, but now he cut in from the left and with his less favoured right foot lashed a shot across Lunin into the top corner. We had the strength not to lose our minds at this reverse. After ten minutes without making further inroads, and with barely ten minutes left on the clock, I sent on Brahim and Joselu while Tuchel withdrew Musiala and Kane. Mentally, I think that Bayern were already in the final.

What happened next was something that can happen to even the best goalkeepers in such high-pressure games. Vinícius had been giving Kimmich a hard time all game but had nothing to show for it. Now he tried a hopeful shot from just outside the area which pitched just in front of Manuel Neuer. Unbelievably, one of the best goalkeepers in the world, who had already made several saves, allowed the ball to bounce off his chest straight into the path of Joselu, who was following up as all strikers are meant to do.

The teams were level. Now we sensed the possibility of more. The players smelled blood. So much so that two minutes later both our central defenders, with no more Kane to worry about, were found in Bayern's penalty area when a hopeful cross from Vinícius fetched up at the feet of Nacho.

THE SEVENTH TIME, 2022–4

Almost in slow motion he turned this way and that before slipping the ball on the left to Rüdiger, who delivered the perfect cross to Joselu to tap home. 2–1.

Joselu's contribution was a fantastic reflection of the squad. He was the kind of player who, while not playing as much as he would like, never loses confidence and continues to believe that he can offer something to the team. Every club needs a Joselu. His goals were registered to the 88th and the 91st minute. That this final moment of drama had happened yet again is unexplainable. It's something magical. The fans and the atmosphere in the stadium and the great reputation of the club all help. They give Real confidence and can burrow deep into the psyche of visiting teams. As Bayern fans knew from Benzema's high-speed hat-trick two seasons earlier, this is what Real Madrid can do to the opposition. They never ever lose until the final whistle tells them to stop. As Sir Alex used to say, 'We don't lose, we just run out of time.'

To add to the intensity of the drama, Bayern did manage to find the net through Matthijs de Ligt, only for the linesman to raise his flag. It was a controversial decision and Tuchel got so angry he was shown a yellow card. But, even if poorly managed, it was the correct decision.

The statistics suggest that we should not necessarily have managed to fight through three knockout rounds in the way we did. In the six games that took Madrid to the final, our opponents had taken more than 100 shots against us. Much

THE DREAM

more than we had managed against them. And yet Real were on their way to Wembley.

The final would be my third with the club, sixth as a coach, eighth in all, ninth if you include the one I watched from the stand 40 years earlier as a Roma player. I had participated in 32 finals and won 24 of them. It would be my 1,324th game in charge. That's a lot of nervous energy, and it doesn't get any easier just because you have experienced finals before. As we made our preparations, I could not help thinking about the 2005 final in Istanbul. It was the best performance in a Champions League final that any team of mine has ever given, and yet it's the only time I've lost. If my record in the final was good, Real's was even better. Since the European Cup changed format and structure in 1992, they'd won the last eight times they'd got this far.

As usual I tried to influence the result by eating my ritual meal of pasta with a sauce of salmon and broccoli. It's the only superstition I have stuck with, because I have learned to believe that not having that meal brings bad luck. After taking a siesta for an hour, I start thinking about the game. The heartbeat starts to go up towards 120 beats per minute just at the moment I begin the team talk and it doesn't go down again until the whistle goes for the start of the match.

Our opponents were Borussia Dortmund. Their coach, Edin Terzić, had been at Wembley as a supporter the last time the final was there in 2013. They had a hard journey to the final, emerging from a group with Paris Saint-Germain,

THE SEVENTH TIME, 2022–4

Milan and Newcastle, then beating PSV, Atlético and PSG. They weren't favourites, nor was the side full of superstars, and they had finished only fifth in the Bundesliga that season. But we knew they could be hard to beat. Of the players to look out for, the one I knew personally was Mats Hummels from my time at Bayern. In central midfield was Marcel Sabitzer and up front was the burly centre-forward Niclas Füllkrug. And then there was Jadon Sancho, the winger back on loan from Manchester United. It was also going to be an emotional day for Bellingham. Only a year earlier most of the opposition had been his team-mates.

The big news in the media was my selection of Courtois in goal. He had spent the whole season out but in two games back before the final he proved his fitness. It was hard for Lunin, but my job was to pick the very best team. It was a risk, but a risk I was prepared to take. Courtois, when fit, is the best. As a team we also knew that this was to be the last game that Toni Kroos would play for the club before he retired.

What I loved about this squad was the lack of big egos. They were a humble group who were easy to manage, no matter how much money they were paid or how many trophies they'd won. Or how old or young they were. And they worked hard. Both of these qualities are, for me, non-negotiable.

I sent out a team that mixed experience at the back with youth further up the pitch. The average age of the back six – Courtois, Mendy, Nacho, Rüdiger, Carvajal and Kroos – was

31. The average age of the front five – Camavinga, Valverde, Bellingham, Rodrygo and Vinícius – was only 22. That selection was a perfect expression of my belief that winning has to start with not conceding. The back six must provide the foundation of comfort and safety and solidity. The front five have the freedom to be creative and innovative.

Not that we did much that was either innovative or creative in the first half. Possession was shared equally, and yet Dortmund were all over us. I was grateful to have Courtois. They created chance after chance, more than half of them on target. The closest they came was when Füllkrug broke through and hit a post. I thought we were just a bit lazy, with only two attempts on goal. We certainly didn't look like European champions elect. Dortmund were playing a fantastic game in transition that made us lose our balance. They were going wide and trying to go in behind us. But once we got to half-time, the feeling was that they had let us off the hook.

Back in the dressing room we had a team discussion. I didn't need to get angry, and there was no call for a motivational speech. I just wanted to clarify a few things because it was obvious that, although it was still 0–0, we were being well beaten. But I thought that we had seen the best of them. The team was confident that Dortmund had missed their chance to kill us off and now the tables could be turned. I voiced my opinion that we were overloaded in midfield and suggested moving to a 4–3–3 so that we wouldn't lose so much possession in their half. The senior players chipped in that they

THE SEVENTH TIME, 2022–4

were finding it hard to press and so we came up with a solution. We put Rodrygo on the right, Valverde back in midfield and moved Camavinga to the left. It made us more compact. I also pushed Vinícius further forward because I knew he could be the difference. After an hour we made a final tweak and moved Bellingham to play as a withdrawn nine.

> Davide Ancelotti, Carlo's son and number-one assistant, explained that this half-time process, in the heat of a Champions League final, was normal.
>
> *On the touchline we had decided that there had to be change because Dortmund had been the better team. The manager doesn't necessarily impose a solution. I think it was more like a sort of a question that he posed to the group, like, 'What if we switch a little bit, like it's because I think we have this problem, but do you agree – do you agree with this idea?' He thought the problem was that we were overloaded in midfield, so we needed to change the system and go with three midfielders, to switch to a 4–3–3, Bellingham, Kroos, Camavinga. So, he [Bellingham] would hold on to that left side of the midfield and Vinicius to hold wide on the left with Valverde on the right and Rodrygo as a nine. This would give us stability.*
>
> *That was the conversation at half-time. It was from a discussion around the manager's thoughts and with the input of the key players, the captain [Nacho], also the senior players,*

THE DREAM

like Carvajal and Kroos. Their view was that we needed one more player in midfield. Kroos said that we couldn't press them, which meant that we had to wait a little bit back. This feedback made the manager adjust his idea a little bit. As a result of the initial discussion, he built on the idea and made slight adjustments and then re-presented the idea so that it came from the group, and he asked the group if they agreed, and they agreed.

Everybody agreed but the interesting thing was that it still wasn't working properly and after about ten minutes we changed again, from the touchline, obviously with no discussion with the players. We put Bellingham as a withdrawn nine, Rodrygo on the right, Valverde back in midfield and moved Camavinga on the left. Then it started to work a little bit better in the second half. They started to lose some balls. They were tiring as well.

Jude Bellingham, as the new kid on the block, provided an interesting take on the half-time 'conversations'.

I don't remember much changing at all at half-time. I do remember Carlo said, 'Well, we've seen the best of them now, so if they haven't scored and we know what they're doing – they're trying to go in behind, they're trying to go wide and have Sancho go one-on-one. Just nullify that and we're there or thereabouts.'

THE SEVENTH TIME, 2022-4

I remember Dani [Carvajal] saying something like, 'If they haven't killed us with that much dominance, they're not going to kill us at all; we can kill them now.' I feel when we play you have to put the knife in our heart and twist it, otherwise it's not enough. It's not enough against Madrid. The knife has to go straight through and come out the other end, otherwise we'll always come back and kill you.

That half-time, in the biggest game I'd ever played in, summed up what makes Carlo special. He'll never say anything that feels like cliché – he'll give you exactly what the game needs, whether it's 'Be more compact,' 'Jude you're going to have to come slightly more narrow – when the ball's here you're going to go here.' It would never be just more and more 'Come on, come on.' It's not motivational, it's informational.

He will never waste time on the basic things you should already know. He doesn't waste any time with that. It's really concise. It's like exactly what you need, and that for me, is key. Keep it simple. For example, tactically, it ultimately comes down to simplicity for Carlo – get the defensive structure right, I have a team where we'll score goals. If you keep a zero, we'll win the game – simple as that.

I feel like some modern coaches come with so many instructions because they feel like they've got to do more than other coaches. They almost want to be puppet masters.

THE DREAM

It worked. In the second half everything changed. Dortmund started to concede more possession. The big difference was Vinícius managing to break loose from the attentions of Dortmund's Ryerson. As the season progressed I had come to understand that he does not want to play through the centre, and I wouldn't want to force him, so instead I gave him freedom. He was always fantastic one-on-one, but I helped him to be more effective when he came inside. When he's wide he has to beat two people to get a shot in. Moving into the middle he could score with one touch. He did this more and more as the season progressed. Now in the second half we saw both versions.

Early in the half he went on a dangerous run and was fouled outside the box. Kroos's free kick was our first attempt on target and required a smart save. The tide was turning. We started to win corners. In the 73rd minute Vinícius won one on the left, which brought about another. Kroos curled an in-swinging cross onto the head of Carvajal, our shortest defender, who glanced it from the near post across the keeper and in. It was a run across the face of the Dortmund goal that Carvajal had made only minutes earlier and nearly scored. Allowed a second chance, he did not pass it up. Ten minutes later the final was over. Bellingham could have doubled the lead when Camavinga pulled a ball back on the left and set him up. His first touch was a little heavy and his shot drifted wide. But we could feel a goal was coming. Their keeper made good saves from Kroos and Camavinga, then

THE SEVENTH TIME, 2022–4

Nacho. Then Ian Maatsen, who was one of Dortmund's best players on the day, made a sloppy square pass across his own back line, looking for Hummels. Bellingham pounced, pushed it left into the path of Vinícius and started raising his arms to celebrate even before his team-mate cued up a shot and scored. Both goals epitomised the Madrid aura, the feeling that something will happen from somewhere although we are never quite sure how it will happen and from where.

Although there were seven minutes until full-time, I felt that the game was basically over. But thanks to the memory of Istanbul, I never accept victory except maybe when we're four up with three minutes to go. So I couldn't relax.

In the 85th minute I took off Kroos and sent on Modrić. One club legend for another. I gave Kroos a big hug and a pat on the back as he left the pitch as a Real Madrid player for the last time. Joselu replaced Bellingham. Two minutes later Füllkrug scored with a powerful header, and I was relieved to see the flag of the assistant referee call offside. Militão came on for Rodrygo, Vázquez for Vinícius. In that second half we had 11 attempts on goal. Five were on target and two went in. Real Madrid's efficiency had resurfaced at just the right time. There was something particularly special about this title. It was the culmination of a season in which some of the squad began as apprentices and grew into champions, while others began as champions and grew into legends. And on a tactical level I was proud of the adjustments we were able to make across the season. We adjusted to the loss of three key players to injury in Courtois, Alaba and Eder Militão. Also, over the summer we had lost Benzema, which meant that we had to use a system that had no genuine striker. No matter, Bellingham could be a goal-scoring attacking midfielder, but also with defensive responsibilities, while Vinícius and Rodrygo, both normally wingers, were the twin points of a 4–3–1–2 formation with the freedom to move out wide. When we needed to be more defensive we could revert to 4–4–2. As the season progressed the incoming players, as well as the incumbents, clearly understood their interlocking roles, reinforcing how tactically flexible we could be. By overcoming all the problems, we were able to win a La Liga/Champions League double, all due to a perfect combination of the talents, attitude and commitment of all the players and staff. Real is a football club with a great weight of history and tradition. This is very important to those who wear this shirt. But for me, before everything, the team is a family. That is why at the final whistle I was as emotional as I've ever been after conquering Europe as a player or as a manager. The seventh time – honestly it felt as good as the first in 1989, as meaningful as the third in 2002, as important as La Décima in 2014. Some of that side was still with us, still winning, ten years on. I rushed to embrace my wife, Mariann, in the crowd.

THE SEVENTH TIME, 2022–4

Then I joined my fantastic players to share in their exhilaration and their achievement. And finally, I could enjoy a feeling that as a coach you only know at moments like this.

The dream had come true, again. A short time to enjoy the success, to rest and recover and to prepare to pursue the Dream once more next season.

Epilogue

After the euphoria of the 2023–4 season and especially winning my seventh Champions' League title, we had only two months in which to sit down and plan for the 2024–5 season and to start dreaming of an eighth Champions League trophy. What would we need to do to repeat last season's successes? There was the excitement at the arrival of one of the world's best players, Kylian Mbappé, but there was also the disappointment of losing the quality, experience and leadership provided by Toni Kroos and Nacho. We would also have to closely monitor the playing time of Luka Modrić, although at times he did not seem to need a rest. It was particularly difficult to lose Kroos. At 34 he was still in his prime and was the controller of the team's rhythm.

But as the reigning champions and with the high expectations of the fans, the media and pretty much everybody else, it was thought that by adding Mbappé to an already Champion team, things could only get better. I still thought that with a little luck we had the quality to carry on where we had left off and fulfil the expectations being heaped upon us. But it turned out that we weren't that lucky. Very quickly, Dani Carvajal and Éder Militão joined Alaba as long-term absentees, although on the plus side, it did enable us to call up Raúl Asencio, a 21-year-old academy graduate, who proved himself as a genuine first-choice option alongside Rüdiger.

Our US tour allowed us to get the players in good shape for the upcoming season and we could begin thinking about tactical issues when we got back from the United States. Our first competitive game of the new season was the UEFA Super Cup against Atalanta just four days before our first league match in Mallorca.

Against Atalanta I was able to field what was probably my preferred starting 11. We did not look far off from where we had finished the previous season. We were solid at the back, conceding only two shots on target, and threatening up front with twice as many shots as Atalanta and with a good conversion rate. A good start.

The games leading up to the first Champions League match were also solid. We scored eight times in the four matches and conceded only one. The first game of the new format Champions League arrived in mid-September, at home against Stuttgart. It was the first game under the new 'Swiss Model' structure, which meant playing eight matches against eight *different* opponents. We had to finish in the top eight to qualify automatically for the knockout stages.

It wasn't clear what the best strategy would be with the new structure. Of course, you wanted to win every game, but there was a big difference in playing Liverpool away rather than at home. Like all the clubs, we were finding our way with the new format.

EPILOGUE

We didn't play our best against Stuttgart, but we won. Possibly we could have worked harder on possession, but you have to choose between building or playing vertically. If we played for possession we would not have scored the first goal, which was from a long pass from Tchouaméni. Real Madrid fans had become used to our style – not a lot of touches but intensity, urgency and pace; not wasting too much time in reaching the opponent's goal. We also had players with a lot of strength and speed, especially on the ball, and we had to take advantage of that.

Clearly, we had not reached our best but that is normal early in what is always a demanding calendar and more so this first season with extra Champions League matches as well as the various Super Cups played across the globe. Nevertheless, we were gradually getting back to our best, but then we stumbled in the second Champions League match away to Lille (LOSC).

The media saw our loss away to the French side as an upset, but Lille is a good team and actually finished the league section of the new structure in seventh place, beating Atlético 3–1 in Madrid and qualifying automatically for the round of 16. On the day, they played better and deserved to win.

In the next match we beat Dortmund with an impressive scoreline (5–2) by playing some great football and scoring some great goals. We were a little sluggish early on and were 2–0 down in thirty minutes but that woke us up and we were level on the hour with two goals in two minutes and we went in front when Lucas Vázquez scored with a fierce angled drive with just seven minutes left. As usual we showed great mental resilience.

Up next in the Champions League were my old team, AC Milan. We lost a very close game, but that's football. When you think everything is perfect, you fall. The good thing about football is that you can always get back up.

We worked hard to rebalance the team that had become unbalanced by the injury absences of Carvajal, Alaba and Militão in particular. Players such as Lucas Vázquez, Tchouaméni, Bellingham and the ever-dependable Valverde all had to play in unfamiliar roles to help the team. To their credit they all knuckled down without complaint.

Liverpool away at Anfield were next up and although we lost the game the old resilience was back. Liverpool just managed to edge us in the areas in which we usually excelled – pace, power, intensity, clinical finishing.

Against Atalanta we managed to get back on the winning road. We had greater control in front of our defence and went ahead early. We were pulled back just before half-time but came back in a three-minute burst midway through the second half. As usual, the good news was that we were reacting to adversity well.

The defeat of Atalanta was not perfect, but some of our efficiency had returned. However, although we had managed to beat the Italian team, we were not out of the woods

EPILOGUE

in the Champions League. During January we had two more games still to play, against Salzburg (matchday 7) and Brest (matchday 8), and we had to win them both to be sure of qualifying for the play-offs, at least. Fortunately, we were able to overcome Salzburg and Brest in those remaining fixtures without too many problems, although we hadn't managed to recover from our losses sufficiently to have qualified automatically for the knockout stage, but we were still alive.

In the additional play-off game we had to play in order to reach the round of 16, we drew our old adversaries, Manchester City, who had been having a bad time themselves, losing three of their games and finishing joint-bottom of the group of those not eliminated at the first hurdle. It was probably a good time to meet them.

The first leg in Manchester followed a similar pattern to our previous matches with City. Both teams seem to score when the other in in the ascendancy. We started really well then conceded in 20 minutes but replied on the hour. Haaland looked to have won the game for City with ten minutes to go but with just four minutes left we equalised again and then Jude Bellingham added the winner two minutes into injury time.

The second leg at the Bernabéu was much more relaxed from the moment that Asencio played a fantastic long-distance pass over the City back line for Mbappé to race clear and lob the ball over the City keeper. He added two more as we looked close to our best.

THE DREAM

The draw for the last 16 set up a Madrid derby and in true derby fashion both legs were attritional battles. The first leg at the Bernabéu was decided by three brilliant goals, two from us and one from them. The second leg was bound to be attritional from the moment Atlético scored after only 30 seconds. With both teams level on aggregate it seemed inevitable that the tie would end in a penalty shoot-out, which it did. However, nobody could have predicted the bizarre moment that arguably decided 210+ minutes of football. On the fourth penalty Atlético's Julián Alvarez slipped as he struck the ball, but it clipped his non-kicking foot on route to the goal. VAR disallowed it – double touch. We were through and looked forward to a quarter-final tie with Arsenal.

We fielded a team that still had key players playing out of position but with the job of navigating our way through the first leg at the Emirates in London unscathed and finishing the job at the Bernabéu. Our back four consisted of Rüdiger and Asencio in the centre with Alaba on the left and Valverde on the right. For 45 minutes it was working. The game was evenly balanced but, on the hour, those tiny margins on which games are decided began to turn in Arsenal's favour. David Alaba, still not fully fit, was just a little over eager when tracking Bukayo Saka and conceded a free kick 20 yards out. The wall was maybe misaligned by as little as 50cm and Declan Rice exploited it. Suddenly the atmosphere became supercharged, and the Arsenal players grew in stature. A second Rice set-piece goal followed soon after. Arsenal were

EPILOGUE

better than us in that last 20 minutes and as we tried to get at least one goal back, we conceded a third. With the three-goal advantage, the tie had turned from being challenging to requiring another miracle in the Bernabéu – the Dream was still alive but hanging by a thread.

One week later the Dream was over for this year. This time Arsenal did not attack us but sat deep with only half the attempts, half the attacks and 40 per cent of the possession but they had more shots on target and more goals on the counter – everything we were famous for, but not on that night. Arsenal had out-Madrided us.

After the Arsenal game the final matches of the season were difficult, but they were the reality. Such times are sent to keep you humble, just in case you thought you were special. Without humility, there's not much you can do.

What was special for me was achieving my Champions League dreams with two of the greatest clubs in world football. Eventually, I would leave both, but they will both always be in my heart. How could I be anything other than grateful that between them both clubs gave me the opportunity to win seven Champions League titles?

My Champions League journey, from that first day watching Roma lose on penalties to the Arsenal game this season, has given me wonderful times, but every phase in life comes to an end to enable the next phase to begin. How lucky am I that my next phase includes the dream of winning the World Cup with the greatest national team in World Cup history?

THE DREAM

My job now is to make Brazil champions again; I accept that, and I'm convinced we can achieve it. To do that I have to make the most of the huge amount of quality that Brazil has by bringing that quality together. The World Cup is different from even the Champions League; it's a feeling with a country behind it, and that's why it always caught my attention.

It is my honour to lead the Seleção. I have always had a connection with Brazil through the players I have played with such as Falcão and Cerezo at Roma; also, with those I have coached such as Ronaldo, Rivaldo, Kaká, Marcelo, Cafu, Casemiro, Richarlison and, most recently with Vinícius Júnior, Rodrygo, Militão and Endrick.

The day I arrived in Brazil, I saw a placard that said, *Welcome Ancelotti, you're the man!* I guess it meant, 'you're the person to bring home the World Cup', and that's the person I want to be. The dream of every Brazilian is for Brazil to become champions again. Now it is my dream also and I will try to deliver that dream by giving it everything I've got. It is a great responsibility, but what a wonderful challenge to have – winning the World Cup with Brazil.

THE 1988–9 SEASON

Road to the Final

First round – 1st leg: Levski 0 – Milan 2

First round – 2nd leg: Milan 5 – Levski 2

Second round – 1st leg: Milan 1 – Red Star Belgrade 1

Second round – 2nd leg: Red Star Belgrade (2) 1 – Milan (4) 1

Quarter-finals – 1st leg: Bremen 0 – Milan 0

Quarter-finals – 2nd leg: Milan 1 – Bremen 0

Semi-finals – 1st leg: Real Madrid 1 – Milan 1

Semi-finals – 2nd leg: Milan 5 – Real Madrid 0

Final: Milan 4 – Steaua Bucharest 0

The line-up against Steaua Bucharest

1	Galli (GK)	7	Donadoni
2	Tassotti	8	Rijkaard
3	Maldini	9	Van Basten
4	Colombo	10	Gullit
5	Costacurta	11	Ancelotti
6	Baresi (C)		

THE 1989–90 SEASON

Road to the Final

First round – 1st leg: Milan 4 – HJK 0
First round – 2nd leg: HJK 0 – Milan 1

Second round – 1st leg: Milan 2 – Real Madrid 0
Second round – 2nd leg: Real Madrid 1 – Milan 0

Quarter-finals – 1st leg: Mechelen 0 – Milan 0
Quarter-finals – 2nd leg: Milan 2 – Mechelen 0

Semi-finals – 1st leg: Milan 1 – Bayern Munich 0
Semi-finals – 2nd leg: Bayern Munich 2 – Milan 1

Final: Milan 1 – Benfica 0

The line-up against Benfica

1	Galli (GK)	7	Ancelotti
2	Tassotti	8	Rijkaard
3	Maldini	9	Van Basten
4	Colombo	10	Gullit
5	Costacurta	11	Evani
6	Baresi (C)		

THE 2002–3 SEASON

Road to the Final

First group stage

Matchday 1: Milan 2 – Lens 1
Matchday 2: Deportivo 0 – Milan 4

Matchday 3: Bayern Munich 1 – Milan 2
Matchday 4: Milan 2 – Bayern Munich 1

Matchday 5: Lens 2 – Milan 1
Matchday 6: Milan 1 – Deportivo 2

Second group stage

Matchday 7: Milan 1 – Real Madrid 0
Matchday 8: Borussia Dortmund 0 – Milan 1

Matchday 9: Milan 1 – Lokomotiv Moscow 0
Matchday 10: Lokomotiv Moscow 0 – Milan 1

Matchday 11: Real Madrid 3 – Milan 1
Matchday 12: Milan 0 – Borussia Dortmund 1

Knockout stage

Quarter-finals – 1st leg: Ajax 0 – Milan 0
Quarter-finals – 2nd leg: Milan 3 – Ajax 2

APPENDIX

Semi-finals – 1st leg: Milan 0 – Inter 0

Semi-finals – 2nd leg: Inter 1 – Milan 1

Final: Juventus (2) 0 – Milan (3) 0

The line-up against Juventus

12	Dida (GK)	10	Rui Costa
3	Maldini (C)	13	Nesta
4	Kaladze	19	Costacurta
7	Shevchenko	20	Seedorf
8	Gattuso	21	Pirlo
9	Inzaghi		

THE 2006–7 SEASON

Road to the Final

Group stage

Matchday 1: Milan 3 – AEK Athens 0
Matchday 2: Lille 0 – Milan 0

Matchday 3: Anderlecht 0 – Milan 1
Matchday 4: Milan 4 – Anderlecht 1

Matchday 5: AEK Athens 1 – Milan 0
Matchday 6: Milan 0 – Lille 2

Knockout stage

Round of 16 – 1st leg: Celtic 0 – Milan 0
Round of 16 – 2nd leg: Milan 1 – Celtic 0

Quarter-finals – 1st leg: Milan 2 – Bayern Munich 2
Quarter-finals – 2nd leg: Bayern Munich 0 – Milan 2

Semi-finals – 1st leg: Manchester United 3 – Milan 2
Semi-finals – 2nd leg: Milan 3 – Manchester United 0

Final: Milan 2 – Liverpool 1

APPENDIX

The line-up against Liverpool

- 1   Dida (GK)
- 3   Maldini (C)
- 8   Gattuso
- 9   Inzaghi
- 10   Seedorf
- 13   Nesta
- 18   Jankulovski
- 21   Pirlo
- 22   Kaká
- 23   Ambrosini
- 44   Oddo

THE 2013–14 SEASON

Road to the Final

Group stage

Matchday 1: Galatasaray 1 – Real Madrid 6
Matchday 2: Real Madrid 4 – Copenhagen 0

Matchday 3: Real Madrid 2 – Juventus 1
Matchday 4: Juventus 2 – Real Madrid 2

Matchday 5: Real Madrid 4 – Galatasaray 1
Matchday 6: Copenhagen 0 – Real Madrid 2

Knockout stage

Round of 16 – 1st leg: Schalke 1 – Real Madrid 6
Round of 16 – 2nd leg: Real Madrid 3 – Schalke 1

Quarter-finals – 1st leg: Real Madrid 3 – Borussia Dortmund 0
Quarter-finals – 2nd leg: Borussia Dortmund 2 – Real Madrid 0

Semi-finals – 1st leg: Real Madrid 1 – Bayern Munich 0
Semi-finals – 2nd leg: Bayern Munich 0 – Real Madrid 4

Final: Real Madrid 4 – Atlético Madrid 1

APPENDIX

The line-up against Atlético Madrid

- 1 Casillas (GK) (C)
- 2 Varane
- 4 Ramos
- 5 Fábio Coentrão
- 6 Khedira
- 7 Ronaldo
- 9 Benzema
- 11 Bale
- 15 Carvajal
- 19 Modrić
- 22 Di María

THE 2021–2 SEASON

Road to the Final

Group stage

Matchday 1: Inter Milan 0 – Real Madrid 1
Matchday 2: Real Madrid 1 – Sheriff 2

Matchday 3: Shakhtar 0 – Real Madrid 5
Matchday 4: Real Madrid 2 – Shakhtar 1

Matchday 5: Sheriff 0 – Real Madrid 3
Matchday 6: Real Madrid 2 – Inter Milan 0

Knockout stage

Round of 16 – 1st leg: Paris Saint-Germain 1 – Real Madrid 0
Round of 16 – 2nd leg: Real Madrid 3 – Paris Saint-Germain 1

Quarter-finals – 1st leg: Chelsea 1 – Real Madrid 3
Quarter-finals – 2nd leg: Real Madrid 2 – Chelsea 3

Semi-finals – 1st leg: Manchester City 4 – Real Madrid 3
Semi-finals – 2nd leg: Real Madrid 3 – Manchester City 1

Final: Liverpool 0 – Real Madrid 1

APPENDIX

The line-up against Liverpool

- 1 Courtois (GK)
- 2 Carvajal
- 3 Éder Militão
- 4 Alaba
- 8 Kroos
- 9 Benzema (C)
- 10 Modrić
- 14 Casemiro
- 15 Valverde
- 20 Vinícius Júnior
- 23 Mendy

THE 2023–4 SEASON

Road to the Final

Group stage

Matchday 1: Real Madrid 1 – Union Berlin 0
Matchday 2: Napoli 2 – Real Madrid 3

Matchday 3: Braga 1 – Real Madrid 2
Matchday 4: Real Madrid 3 – Braga 0

Matchday 5: Real Madrid 4 – Napoli 2
Matchday 6: Union Berlin 2 – Real Madrid 3

Knockout stage

Round of 16 – 1st leg: Leipzig 0 – Real Madrid 1
Round of 16 – 2nd leg: Real Madrid 1 – Leipzig 1

Quarter-finals – 1st leg: Real Madrid 3 – Manchester City 3
Quarter-finals – 2nd leg: Manchester City (3) 1 – Real Madrid (4) 1

Semi-finals – 1st leg: Bayern Munich 2 – Real Madrid 2
Semi-finals – 2nd leg: Real Madrid 2 – Bayern Munich 1

Final: Borussia Dortmund 0 – Real Madrid 2

APPENDIX

The line-up against Borussia Dortmund

[1]	Courtois (GK)	[11]	Rodrygo
[2]	Carvajal	[12]	Camavinga
[5]	Bellingham	[15]	Valverde
[6]	Nacho (C)	[22]	Rüdiger
[7]	Vinícius Júnior	[23]	Mendy
[8]	Kroos		

Acknowledgements

Without the players I played with and coached, and the colleagues I worked with, none of my successes would have been possible.